CARL JUNG

Wounded Healer of the Soul

CARL JUNG

Wounded Healer of the Soul

Claire Dunne

WATKINS
Sharing Wisdom Since 1893

Published in association with the
Shelley & Donald Rubin Foundation, New York

Carl Jung – Wounded Healer of the Soul
Claire Dunne

This edition first published in the UK and USA in 2015,
in association with the Shelley & Donald Rubin Foundation, New York,
by Watkins, an imprint of Watkins Media Limited,
19 Cecil Court
London WC2N 4EZ

enquiries@watkinspublishing.com

First published in 2000 by Parabola Books, USA

Managing Editor: Sandra Rigby
Senior Editor: Fiona Robertson
Designers: Studio 31, Luana Gobbo, Gail Jones
Picture Research: Miriam Faugno and Emma Copestake
Production: Uzma Taj

A CIP record for this book is available from the British Library

ISBN: 978-1-78028-831-4

10 9 8 7 6 5 4 3

Typeset in Gill Sans
Colour reproduction by XY Digital Limited
Printed in China

www.watkinspublishing.com

PAGE 2: *The Alchemist*; manuscript page from Salomon Trismosin, *Splendor Solis*, 1582.

Watkins gratefully acknowledges the financial support of the Shelley & Donald Rubin Foundation, New York, in making possible the publication of this new edition of *Carl Jung – Wounded Healer of the Soul*. Claire Dunne's outstanding contribution to Jungian scholarship has been widely acclaimed by both academics and professionals, and continues to educate and inform a wider readership. The book derives its authority from a unique combination of primary source material, inspirational artworks and the author's compelling insight and analysis.

CONTENTS

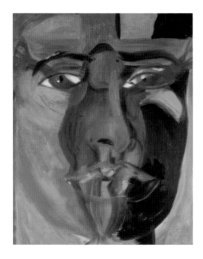

FOREWORD

C.G. JUNG: UNDERSTANDING THE WORLD

Inside and outside, the psyche and the world: when C.G. Jung explored the first, he also provided us with a new understanding of the other. We read Jung, discover the collective unconscious, and become aware of our shared humanity; we understand the elements of our personality and begin to see why we – and others – behave as we do. We read the account of Jung's own tortured journey in *The Red Book*, and it becomes frighteningly clear that there is no personal growth without suffering, and that there can be no progress without personal growth.

For a while, in the 1970s and '80s, Jung was fashionable in the United States. His categories became buzzwords, and thus, too often, easy and fallacious explanations; but, at least, many people felt the need to look in and reach a new depth of understanding. That has changed; a new, mechanistic kind of behaviorism is now the fashion; analysis is held to be too slow, too expensive, too inconvenient. A quick, easy, and cheap modification is thought best; and the result is a proliferation of often violent reactions which are neither understood nor really felt – a sense that we live in an uncontrollable and often painful world.

We have indeed followed a curious path. The great thinkers of the Enlightenment rejected the trammels of the theologians. As they removed the endless prohibitions of traditional religions, they viewed the world in the bright light of Reason, and Science prospered. A century later, Freud officialized the existence of the unconscious, and its crucial importance in determining our feelings and our behavior; but his view was finally too reductionist. It was left for Jung to bring together culture and the unconscious, history and the archetypes; and as he did so, he provided us with the key to many mysteries – and also with a way to improve ourselves, or, more exactly, to resist unpleasant manifestations of our repressions by becoming who we really are.

Tragically, not enough people, these days, read Jung, but Claire Dunne's *Carl Jung – Wounded Healer of the Soul* may attract some converts. Admittedly, the sight of Jung's collected works can be daunting; nor is every one of his books readily accessible to the uninitiated. Even so, there is plenty we can read, and knowing about Jung's own journey is a perfect introduction. It is not just that we sympathize and wish him success: his struggle awakens in us curiosity and emulation. We may not wish to suffer as he did, but then we don't have to: we can enjoy the fruit of his labors, learn from his discoveries, and turn it all to our own psychological profit. To understand ourselves better is, of course, deeply rewarding, but there is more: those buried, unhealed wounds can now be seen, treated, and finally made harmless. And then comes the final step toward individuation: the discovery of who we really are, the opening of all those possibilities which exist because we are, finally, in touch with our talents and ourselves.

The drama and eloquence of *Carl Jung – Wounded Healer of the Soul* would be enough to make us want to read it, but it is not just an account of the life of a great man. As Dunne tells us about Jung, she also tells us about analytical psychology; in fact, she offers us just the introduction into the world of Jung most likely to make us want to learn more. And that is the first step to seeing through the many illusions that cause deep and lasting unhappiness.

Understanding ourselves is also a tool for understanding the world. Aberrant, even destructive behavior on the part of nations and their leaders can often be understood in terms of psychology: if they are in the grip of an archetype, they are likely to forge blindly and destructively ahead – and if we understand that, we are better able to deal with them. And then there is history. What was confusing or obscure becomes clear, just as what was opaque in ourselves is now transparent. We leave a world of dark, incomprehensible mysteries for a transparent, accessible, comprehensible universe; and that releases our creative potential even as it provides the deep satisfaction we experience when we finally understand.

Claire Dunne is thus doing us an enormous favor. By introducing us to Jung and to his *Weltanschauung*, she provides a necessary impetus. After reading *Carl Jung – Wounded Healer of the Soul*, many will feel the need to move on to Jung's own books. As light begins to dawn, as we begin to see, to understand, to yearn for more clarity, we are also on the way to that magic formula that transmutes lead to gold.

OLIVIER BERNIER

PREFACE TO THE NEW EDITION

This book tells the story of the evolving personal and spiritual journey of Carl Gustav Jung, whose psychological legacy is still coming into its own as a profound influence on the world.

In 1913, Jung, then a prominent international figure in the newly formed psychiatric field, underwent a psychic death and rebirth, out of which emerged his own psychology. It was the major journey of his life.

Jung's *The Red Book*, containing his record of this inner process as it happened, was released for publication in 2009 after decades of speculation as to its contents.

The article that I wrote for the *Life After Death* edition of *Parabola* magazine gives a condensed sense of what *The Red Book* contains. It supplements and enlarges upon what is covered in this book's Part One – "Wounded". The article is reproduced here as an essential blueprint of the consciousness Jung lived, and the inner experiences he had, worked with, and poured forth as universal message for the rest of his life.

CARL JUNG'S *THE RED BOOK*

> The knowledge of death came to me that night…. I went into the inner death and saw that outer dying is better than inner death. And I decided to die outside and live within…. I turned away and sought the place of the inner life!

C.G. Jung, *The Red Book*

The Red Book, an epic chapter in the life of C.G. Jung, is now available to us forty-eight years after his death. This fabled red-leather-bound volume, which Jung initially called *Liber Novus* (New Book), echoes a medieval manuscript in its calligraphic text and richly toned symbolic paintings. It reveals a process that was primal in its energies and labyrinthine in its journey, one that became the genesis of his psychology, "the numinous beginning that contained everything", he wrote in 1957, four years before he died.

Cary Baynes, a former patient who was asked by Jung to transcribe the text, called it a "record of the passage of the universe through the soul of a man." It records the search, experiences and initial findings of a man who at age forty had, by his own account, "achieved honour, power, wealth, knowledge and every human happiness," yet had somehow lost his soul.

"Meine seele, meine seele, wo bist du?" "My soul, my soul, where are you?" Jung writes in the Black Book series that preceded and was elaborated upon in *The Red Book*. In his introduction to *The Red Book*, editor Sonu Shamdasani, Philemon Professor of Jung History at University College, London, sets this potent work within the context of Jung's time and life.

It began in 1913, the year Jung broke with Freud. Inner experiences were drawing Jung into a way of being not primarily dependent on intellect. There were dreams he didn't understand and then a repeated and dramatic sign – a daylight vision of horrific floods, Europe devastated, rivers of blood, and an inner voice that said: "It will come to pass."

"I thought my mind had gone crazy," wrote Jung. He undertook a psychological self-examination but became stuck. To tap into underlying material, he devised a "boring method" that evolved into "active imagination," which was to become a keystone of his psychology as a means of accessing and penetrating fantasy. From late 1913 to mid-1914, he recorded a relentless avalanche of inner openings, images, and dialogues, material for his "most difficult experiment."

Often these experiences occurred at night in his library, following a day's work with patients, and dinner with family. He sometimes did yoga-type exercises to quell emotional turmoil and empty his consciousness. He then went into the spontaneous fantasies that appeared, as if entering a drama, engaging in conversations with their characters. But he remained uncertain of the meaning and significance of their content. Mental illness was a recurring fear.

"Finally I understood," he wrote in 1914, after the outbreak of World War I. His early symbolic precognitions had been given terrible form. Understanding gave Jung the courage to begin a handwritten draft of his Liber Novis. He transcribed the Black Book material, adding further interpretations of each episode, and often combining these with a lyrical elaboration.

Some snapshot impressions of the book may yield a skeleton of its content. Inner battles take place. In the prophetic opening the Spirit of the Depths spars with the Spirit of the Times in him. The contemporary and changing thinking of Time constantly has to give way to the immemorial and shaping future contained in, and arising from, the Depths.

A spiritual message emerges, a new way for the time we live in today, with Jung becoming the task, interpreter and bearer of it. The teaching is of a new God image – an immanent God who is in everything big and small, dark and light. The paradox in this holds that "the highest truth and the absurd is one and the same thing." Moreover, "the melting together of sense and nonsense produces the supreme meaning"; and "if you marry the ordered to the chaos you produce the divine child." The task is to hold the opposites together, "the goal is not the heights but the center" – the center or Self which can be said as "God in us."

Jung came to believe that "You should be ... not Christians but Christ, otherwise you will be of no use to the coming God." He realized he needed to live all of life in him, God spirit and human animal, together in unity.

In Jung's personal journey his feminine Soul voice battles with him to recognize and balance his own opposites. There is a peeling back of distrust, scorn, judgment, pride, defiance, doubt, confusion, rage, and fear. The need to develop patience – a waiting, enduring, receiving mode as the feminine (or anima) within – is put to him. He discovers that thinking and feeling need each other.

Jung has to face what least he wants to – symbolized as desert, hell, murder, and more, till "nothing human is alien to me." Opposites, he realizes, are brothers: "the other is also in you." Soul counsels acceptance of solitude, the inner loneliness of knowing, uncertainty of path or goal, and fear and possibility of madness as part of his journey. "I believed ... soul knows her own way ... perhaps no one will gain insight from my work. But my soul demands this achievement.... I should be able to do this just for myself, without hope – for the sake of God."

Jung carves his own path, insisting "my path is not your path" and, "to live oneself is to be one's own task." The fantasies deepen in a spiraling journey of recurring, evolving patterns. The horror and the positive aspects of collective human history unfold before him. Soul insists he accept it all. "I feel the things that were and that will be." He initially recoils at the enormous task ahead. "Futurity grows out of me; I do not create it, and yet I do."

A transformative image of a black snake appears, winding up, becoming white and emerging through the mouth of the crucified Christ.

"To give birth to the ancient in a new time is creation," he writes.

"We need it [magic] ... to find the way that we are unable to conceive." Looking for inner help, Jung is "apprenticed" to Philemon, a "guru" figure that first appears in dream as a winged man bearing four keys, and then as archetypal Magician. From him, Jung learns about objective reality beyond the personal. He risks the letting go that is needed to bring together powers that conflict in the soul of man into a true marriage. Reason and understanding must unite with unreason and magic. Unity brings an apparent standstill that is "the forbearing life of eternity, the life of divinity." Yet his inner guidance reveals that the personal "life has yet to begin." This section ends with: "the touchstone is being alone with yourself. This is the way."

The Scrutinies section opens with a devastating self-criticism of the "shadow" side of his state. "If I tame you, beast, I give others the opportunity to tame their beasts." Jung is encouraged by Soul to "be unwavering and create" while a haggard male inner image tells him, "you must bleed for the goal of humanity." As World War I savages on, Jung asks his Soul: "Which depths do you require me to advance to?" The answer: "Forever above yourself and the present."

For nearly a year, the voices of the depths fall silent. Jung writes a draft of his *Liber Novus*. Then the voice of Philemon returns. "Self-willing is not for you. You are the will of the whole.... Draw nearer, enter into the grave of God. The place of your work should be in the vault."

The dead appear to his inner vision and Soul tells him, "The dead demand your expiatory prayers." Jung reluctantly accepts. Soul announces that the "ruler of this world" demands the sacrifice of Jung's fear because he has "been summoned to serve him." "Why must it be me?" protests Jung. "I cannot. I don't want to."

"You possess the word that should not be allowed to remain concealed," declares his Soul.

Philemon, who Jung had felt as "the presence of the good and the beautiful," now appears in priestly robes and gives "Seven Sermons to the Dead" a kind of Gnostic Creation myth, including humanity's role in it.

From Pleroma, unmanifest, infinite, eternal, in which "there is nothing and everything," arises differentiated levels of Creation that are permeated with Pleroma. Pairs of opposites, which are balanced and void in Pleroma, appear as separate in created beings, such as good and evil, sameness and difference. The striving at bottom is for "your own essence" as being.

Everything "created and uncreated" is Pleroma itself, the totality of being. The first manifestation devolving from Pleroma is Abraxas, a god forgotten by mankind, whose state of being is "effect," a paradoxical "improbable probability and unreal reality." It is "force, duration, change" at once. The next level of manifestation is more definite. God is Creation. God is in essence "effective fullness" while Satan, his opposite, is in essence "effective emptiness."

Then there is a multiplicity of gods that act as either heavenly gods that "magnify," or earthly gods that "diminish," the four principal ones being Sun God, Eros, Tree of Life, and Devil. Spirituality and sexuality, "daimon manifestations of the gods," are opposites of the same spectrum, celestial in spirituality, earthly in sexuality. Man and woman "stand under the law" of both in differing ways.

In the last of the "Seven Sermons," Philemon reveals that man "is a gateway through which you pass from the outer world of Gods, daimons and souls into the inner world; out of the greater into the smaller world." In this world "man is Abraxas, the creator and destroyer of his own world," who has a star as his own "guiding God."

Much later, Jung told colleague Aniela Jaffé that the "Seven Sermons to the Dead" was a prelude of what he had to communicate to the world. They are the skeletal nucleus of Jung's psychology, including individuation, the conflict of opposites, and the co-creation of man with the godhead.

Yet, the journey of *The Red Book* continued on. Philemon had a further teaching about man: "You, being, are the eternal moment." Death as shade, and celestial mother in mantle of stars, also appear, requiring further sacrifice from Jung before he can give birth to his stellar child. Jung realizes that "only fidelity to love and voluntary devotion" lead to "my stellar nature, my truest and most innermost self, that simply and singly is."

Finally, a shade (Christ) enters. Philemon kneels to "my master and my brother," telling Christ "your work is incomplete" while man merely imitates his life. "The time has come when each must do his own work of redemption."

By the end, clear lines are drawn between the personal Jung and the inner beings that have appeared throughout, including Elijah, Salome, and earth spirit Ka, in addition to Philemon. In a final tussle with Soul Jung refuses unconditional obedience to the gods. He insists that man is no longer "slave" to them, though "They may devise a service in return." After initial outrage the gods agree. Soul tells Jung: "You have broken the compulsion of the law." Christ (as shade) offers a final word as gift. In accepting light and dark together: "I bring you the beauty of suffering."

In 1916, while he was on military duty, a series of mandala images came to Jung. The first, *Systema Munditotius*, depicts a multilevel relationship of microcosm with macrocosm. Abraxas, "lord of the physical world," is at the bottom; Phanes, golden winged "divine child," is at top. Over time Jung transcribed his work into calligraphic form on parchment, illustrated the text, painted dramatic symbolic images of his journey, and inserted it all into a six-hundred-page folio bound in red leather.

Patients recall seeing it, open, on an easel in his library. Jung counseled them to create their own kind of *Red Book* as a method of dealing with their particular inner processes. Christiana Morgan recalls Jung saying, "You can go to the book, turn over the pages and for you it will be your church – your cathedral – the silent places of your spirit where you will find renewal … for in that book is your soul."

Jung stopped work on *The Red Book* in 1930 when the impact of a Chinese alchemical text, *The Secret of the Golden Flower*, brought him "undreamed of confirmation" of his ideas, and the link between East and West. In 1959, a single handwritten page was added to the book by Jung, reaffirming its contents: "I always knew those experiences contained something precious." It ends in mid-sentence.

The Red Book continues for us as profound insight into the processes of life, into Jung and his work, and the need to honor our own inner lives in our own way.

The above article was published in the Summer 2010 issue of *Parabola* magazine and is reproduced here with kind permission. Four of Jung's *The Red Book* paintings are reproduced in this book (pages 70, 79, 80 and 228). They, and cross-cultural symbolic images, add visual context and beauty to his ideas, and the book.

Part One – "Wounded" takes us through Jung's childhood, medical studies, personal and family life, relationship with Sigmund Freud, and his struggles to become what he was, up to the end of the tumultuous period recorded in *The Red Book*.

Part Two – "Healer" follows the mid-years, a flourishing of professional life, the influence on Jung of travels to native America, Africa, and India, the nucleus of his psychology; along with reminiscences of people who knew him as patients, friends, and colleagues. It closes with the dawning turmoil of World War II and an urgent inner call for him to attend to the retrieval of Western civilization.

Part Three – "Of the Soul" opens with Jung's profound near-death experience at 69, a kind of second initiation. As his personal life began to close down, the great works emerged, including *Answer to Job* and the problem of evil; 'Synchronicity: An Acausal Connecting Principle" and links with nuclear physics; *Mysterium Coniunctionis*, the individual's stages of fusion with the universe and the Source of All; and the reaching to a general public with *Memories, Dreams, Reflections* and *Man and His Symbols*.

I came to Jung as an ordinary reading member of the public who evolved in time to writing this book, and to giving talks and workshops in Jungian strongholds all over the world – something I could never have dreamed of when originally caught by *Memories, Dreams, Reflections* decades earlier.

He seemed to me then like an old friend, a feeling I have never lost.

Two things that reached me most in that autobiographical work were Jung's assertion that the psyche is "by nature religious" and his account of two personalities vying in our person: that which we are by nature and that which we become to fit in with family and social circumstance within our cultural milieu. This interplay of opposites, which Jung found acutely active in himself, is played out in our own lives.

In writing about Jung's life, I wanted him to tell his own story as much as possible. As well as revealing his personality, his correspondence contains the distilled thinking of his work, the words still charged with his enlivening energy. This, and original material from his autobiographical and collected works, provide entry to his world.

Over a long lifetime, and not without difficulty, Jung brought himself into a wholeness of being and he invites this self-realization in others as the essential task of our lives, forged in our own way, leading us to the spiritual underpinnings of our existence. I hope you will find in this account of a complex psycho-spiritual pioneer echoes, promptings, recognitions, inspiration for yourselves in your own life journey.

CLAIRE DUNNE

INTRODUCTION

Carl Jung – Wounded Healer of the Soul is a luminous portrait of a great-souled one, a giant figure of the twentieth century.

As a pioneering psychiatrist, Carl Jung extended his influence across an astonishing spectrum: medicine, psychology, art, literature, religion, science, the humanities. His wide-ranging vision consistently pointed the way for much of what became the Human Potential Movement, depth psychology, a revolution in spiritual understanding, and an inclusive universal view of life and its purpose.

In his own life he was, in many ways, a prototype of the human being still being forged in our time, an archetype of the emerging possible human that I observe struggling into being all over the world. That Jung's work is a vital bridge linking East and West to each other as well as to the North–South shamanic axis contributes immeasurably to this evolutionary development. In this regard he was one of the first to show how many members of European-derived cultures reveling in technique and objective mastery are sadly lacking in a spiritual awareness and subjective complexity found in aboriginal and indigenous cultures belonging to other stages of historical development.

Jung's own individuation process, so beautifully presented here, expresses with remarkable clarity and insight the psychic unfolding of his own transforming journey. This process, tracing as it does a self-realization of the psyche through experiencing its deeper layers and integrating them, brings us into a wholeness of being. It is at this point that we come into our own, our natural state of living equilibrium as earth-rooted and spiritually centered people who recognize the Source of our lives, the Ground of all Being, and are willing and able to serve its purposes in a co-creative manner.

The possible human, as it is breathed into life, lives with a vastly expanded consciousness, which brings with it an armory of human skills and abilities, many-textured, multifaceted, and multidimensional. It is an evolutionary leap comparable to the changeover wrought by speech and writing for our ancestors. That state of being produces a new world, which in turn brings about a new state of being. As we see in this study, Jung embodied many of the aspects of the possible human. He lived fully in his body, had acute senses, was engaged by the world as artist and craftsman, had an excellent memory, thought in inward imageries, and experienced subjective realities as strikingly as he knew objective ones. Consciousness for him was a continuum, the length and breadth of which he could travel at will. Throughout his long life he continued to discover the many cultures of his psyche, studying all manner of knowledge and wisdom that these cultures within provided. He had friends and allies in the inward and imaginal worlds, and taught his patients to discover the same, even to find the archetypal partner and companion of one's depth reality. He regularly journeyed to those source places of his soul, partaking of the everlasting waters of life and spirit. It would seem he lived daily life as spiritual exercise, and his radiance, along with his empathy and down-to-earth presence, affected all who met him. Being more in himself, as this richly telling account shows, he felt and cared more deeply about decay and degradation in the social and moral order. In spite of evidence to the contrary, he recognized others as god-in-hiding, and his vast array of techniques and understanding called them back to their own possible humanity.

This book goes back to Jung's words in order to trace the human and spiritual journey of his long life. It is at the same time a brilliant synthesis of his core work, essentially the approach to the numinous via the path of deep psychological maturity. A series of illuminating reminiscences by friends, colleagues, and the occasionally met round out the fullness of the book's portrait. Author Claire Dunne's sensitivity of feeling for her subject allows us to meet Jung in all his diverse complexity – his contradictions and paradox, human failings and strengths, his greatness and creativity. We meet a man at once transparent to transcendence but also earthy, practical, a craftsman of wood and stone as well as souls.

This book exposes us to vitalizing internal drives that underpinned Jung's life and work, the archetypal energies and mythic sensibilities that permeated him, leaving us with no doubt of their deep spiritual source, the Mystery of Mysteries as he called it, or the Holy Mysterious as a Native American might say. Among the mysteries that Jung illumined in his work, and the ones that have so deeply spoken to me, is that of the mythic foundations of our local life. He showed that life is allied with myth in order that we may advance along an evolutionary path that carries us nearer to the spiritual source and into greater becoming. It is for this that myth remains closer than breathing, nearer than our hands and feet. I think it is built into our very being. Myth is not a no thing, an insubstantial conceptual will o' the wisp. It is coded into the cells and waters, the seas, of the unconscious. It dwells in our little finger and plays along the spine as well as the spirit. It grants us access to the DNA of the human psyche, the source patterns originating in the ground of our being. It gives us the key to our personal and historical existence. Without mythic keys, as Jung continually showed, we would have no culture or religion, no art, architecture, drama, ritual, epic, social customs, or mental disorders. We would have only a gray world, with little if anything calling us forward to that strange and beautiful country that recedes even as we attempt to civilize it.

This joining of local life to great life was one of Jung's most profound achievements. It provides ways of moving from outmoded existence to an amplified life that is at once more cherished and more cherishing. As he wrote, "If we understand and feel that here in this life we already have a link with the infinite, desires and attitudes change. In the final analysis, we count for something only because of the essential we embody…." When we descend into the forgotten knowings of earlier or deeper phases of our existence, we often find hidden potentials, the unfulfilled and unfinished seedings of what we still contain, which myth often disguises as secret helpers or mighty talismans. When the story I am working with involves finding talismans, I lead students into enactments aimed at rediscovering skills they had once known, lost perhaps in childhood – a capacity for art or music, for example, or even a sense of empathy. A psychology with a mythic or sacred base demands that we have the courage both to release old toxicities and diminishments and to gain access to our inner storehouse of capacities and use them to prepare ourselves for the greater agenda – becoming an instrument through which the source may play its great music. But such is necessary if we are to return to everyday life with knowledge gained in the depths that can be put to use to redeem the "unread vision of the higher dream" inherent in both self and society.

As Jung demonstrated, myths have such power because they are full of archetypes. Archetypes are many things – primal forms, codings of the deep unconscious, constellations of psychic energy, patterns of relationship. Our ancestors saw them in the heavens, prayed to them as Mother Earth, Father Ocean, Sister Wind. They were the great relatives from whom we were derived, and they gave us not only our existence, but also prompted our stories, elicited our moral order. Later, they became personified in mythic characters and their stories – the contending brothers, the holy child, the search for the beloved, the heroic journey. As major organs of the psyche, archetypes give us our essential connections, and without them we would lose the gossamer bridge that joins spirit with nature, mind with body, and self with the metabody of the universe. Archetypes, as Jung showed again and again, are organs of Essence, the cosmic blueprints of How It All Works. Because they contain so much, archetypes bewilder analysis and perhaps can only be known by direct experience.

Claire Dunne's book brings Jung vibrantly to life. That she enables us to hear so distinctly the challenge he gives us – to be complete, conscious, and modern human beings – is an accomplishment that I can only applaud.

JEAN HOUSTON

PART ONE

WOUNDED

It is the truth, a force of nature that expresses itself through me – I am only a channel – I can imagine in many instances where I would become sinister to you. For instance, if life had led you to take up an artificial attitude, then you wouldn't be able to stand me, because I am a natural being. By my very presence I crystallize; I am a ferment. The unconscious of people who live in an artificial manner senses me as a danger. Everything about me irritates them, my way of speaking, my way of laughing.

They sense nature.[1]

PRELUDE

When Carl Gustav Jung spoke of himself as "a natural being," he was sixty-six years old. By then he was world-famous and controversial, the first modern psychiatrist to recognize that the human psyche is "by nature religious" and to explore it in depth. A self-described "empiricist" and "healer of the soul," he penetrated the inner reaches of himself and his patients, linked his experience to ancient writings and cultures worldwide, and offered his discoveries to an uncomprehending world.

In a letter he wrote,

The main interest of my work is not concerned with the treatment of neurosis but rather with the approach to the numinous … [which] is the real therapy.[2]

Jung's work teaches that:

- Man needs to become his complete self to live whole.
- God needs man to mirror his creation and help it evolve.
- The whole human being is open to God as co-creator.

People who knew Jung testify that he was a living example of his own psychology. At once human, fallible, and great, he lived in two worlds – earth-rooted and spiritually centered. Both "lives," outer and inner, he saw as the natural state of realized humanity.

Jung's work reflects his life. Of himself he said, "I am the clash of opposites." Throughout a long life he learned to live and reconcile those polarities into a unity of wholeness.

At eighty-four he said of that long trek,

The journey from cloud cuckoo land to reality lasted a long time. In my case Pilgrim's Progress consisted in my having to climb down a thousand ladders until I could reach out my hand to the little clod of earth that I am.[3]

PAGE 20: *Self Portrait*; detail of painting by Francesco Clemente, 1982.
OPPOSITE: Dr. Carl Gustav Jung (1875–1961) in his garden at Küsnacht, Switzerland, 1930.

ABOVE: Jung's parents, Emilie Preiswerk (1848–1923) and Johann Paul Achilles Jung (1842–1896).
Emilie encouraged Jung's interest in the occult; his father taught him Latin.

LEFT: Carl Jung, c. 1882.
Young Carl was an only child until the age of nine.

THE CHILD

Late in life, Jung was deeply involved in compiling his "autobiography." It is this book more than any other that attracts the general public to him. Titled *Memories, Dreams, Reflections*, it tells the reader little of Jung's outer life. Instead the book graphically portrays the geography of his inner landscape as both adult and child.

> While I am writing this I observe a little demon trying to abscond my words and even my thoughts and turning them over into the rapidly flowing river of images, surging from the mists of the past, portraits of a little boy, bewildered and wondering at an incomprehensibly beautiful and hideously profane and deceitful world.[4]

The little boy, for nine years the only child of Parson Paul Jung and his wife Emilie, was born in the small village of Kesswil, Switzerland, in 1875.

> Dim intimations of trouble in my parents' marriage hovered around me. My illness in 1878 must have been connected with a temporary separation of my parents. My mother spent several months in a hospital in Basel, and presumably her illness had something to do with the difficulty in the marriage. An aunt of mine, who was a spinster and some twenty years older than my mother, took care of me. I was deeply troubled by my mother's being away. From then on, I always felt mistrustful when the word "love" was spoken. The feeling I associated with "woman" was for a long time that of innate unreliability. "Father," on the other hand, meant reliability and – powerlessness. That is the handicap I started off with. Later these early impressions were revised; I have trusted men friends and been disappointed by them; and I have mistrusted women and was not disappointed.[5]

An early pattern that stayed with him all his life was an intense love of nature, a direct relationship with plants, animals, earth, rock, mountains, river and lake. A simple rustic lifestyle – and solitude.

> I played alone, and in my own way. Unfortunately I cannot remember what I played; I recall only that I did not want to be

disturbed. I was deeply absorbed in my games and could not endure being watched or judged while I played them.[6]

A childhood friend, Albert Oeri, remembered the impact this had on him.

I suppose I saw Jung for the first time in my life when we were still very small boys. My parents were visiting his, and they wanted their little sons to play together. But it was no use. Carl sat in the middle of a room, busying himself with a little game of ninepins and not taking the least notice of me. Why do I even remember this encounter after some fifty-five years? Probably because I had just never run across such an asocial monster. I was brought up in an exuberantly crowded nursery, where you either played together or got beaten up, but either way you constantly associated with people; he was all by himself – his sister had not yet been born at that time.[7]

Jung's sister Gertrud was born when he was nine, too late and different in temperament to be a companion. The Jung family lived in frugal poverty in an eighteenth-century parsonage. The only manmade beauty in the house was a couple of paintings in a dark room, which delighted the boy. His parents fulfilled community

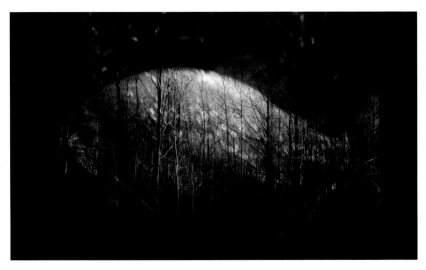

The Fish in the Forest; photograph by Rosalie Winard, 1981.
Nature was the entry to contemplation and experience for Jung.

The Holy Face; painting by Georges Rouault, c. 1946.

The idea of Jesus shifted for Carl as he realized "those that Jesus had taken to himself" were never coming back.

expectations of a pious Protestant minister and his helping wife. Eight of Jung's maternal uncles and two on his father's side were parsons, secure in a conventional world of faith, Bible, and good works. To the sensitive and vulnerable Carl it was a suffocating atmosphere. He became accident-prone in resistance to this form of life. Spiritually, too, it produced unintended results, recorded in *Memories, Dreams, Reflections*:

In the cemetery nearby, the sexton would dig a hole – heaps of brown, upturned earth. Black, solemn men in long frock coats with unusually tall hats and shiny black boots would bring a black box. My father would be there in his clerical gown, speaking in a resounding voice. Women wept. I was told that someone was being buried in this hole in the ground. Certain persons who had been around previously would suddenly no longer be there. Then I would hear that they had been buried, and that Lord Jesus had taken them to himself.

My mother had taught me a prayer which I had to say every evening. I gladly did so....

> *Spread out thy wings, Lord Jesus mild,*
> *And take to thee thy chick, thy child....*

But now I was hearing that Lord Jesus "took" other people to himself as well, and that this "taking" was the same as putting them in a hole in the ground....

I began to distrust Lord Jesus. He lost the aspect of a big, comforting, benevolent bird and became associated with the gloomy black men in frock coats, top hats, and shiny black boots who busied themselves with the black box.[8]

Le Palais des Rideaux; painting by René Magritte, 1928.
The riddle of life and death was represented to the boy at funeral services conducted by his father: "Certain persons who had been around previously would suddenly no longer be there."

At about the same time, Jung encountered the black-robed figure of a Jesuit priest whose appearance traumatized the boy. Impressions of Lord Jesus and the Jesuit combined to build the child's distrust of outer aspects of religion, which resulted in a hatred of going to church.

It was his dream world that connected him to his own internal spiritual network – guiding, informing, signaling the main trends of his life. He later said the early dreams of childhood usually give the tenor of a person's life patterns, often working at several levels at the same time. Jung's earliest remembered dream, at age three or four, was one he kept secret till his mid-sixties. This numinously tinged dream was situated in a meadow not far from his parents' home.

> In the dream I was in this meadow. Suddenly I discovered a dark, rectangular, stone-lined hole in the ground.... I ran forward curiously and peered down into it. Then I saw a stone stairway leading down. Hesitantly and fearfully, I descended. At the bottom was a doorway with a round arch, closed off by a green curtain. It was a big, heavy curtain of worked stuff like brocade, and it looked very sumptuous. Curious to see what might be hidden behind, I pushed it aside. I saw before me in the dim light

a rectangular chamber about thirty feet long. The ceiling was arched and of hewn stone. The floor was laid with flagstones, and in the center a red carpet ran from the entrance to a low platform. On this platform stood a wonderfully rich golden throne. I am not certain, but perhaps a red cushion lay on the seat. It was a magnificent throne, a real king's throne in a fairy tale. Something was standing on it which I thought at first was a tree trunk twelve to fifteen feet high and about one and a half to two feet thick. It was a huge thing, reaching almost to the ceiling. But it was of a curious composition: it was made of skin and naked flesh, and on top there was something like a rounded head with no face and no hair. On the very top of the head was a single eye, gazing motionlessly upward.

It was fairly light in the room, although there were no windows and no apparent source of light. Above the head, however, was an aura of brightness. The thing did not move, yet I had the feeling that it might at any moment crawl off the throne like a worm and creep toward me. I was paralyzed with terror. At that moment I heard from outside and above me my mother's voice. She called out, "Yes, just look at him. That is the man-eater!" That intensified my terror still more, and I awoke sweating and scared to death.[9]

What was he to make of it? The dream haunted him for decades, its meaning discovered bit by bit over the years as he explored ancient writings and religions, the primal cultures of today and of prehistory.

The phallus ... a subterranean god "not to be named"

Celtic stone figure, Holzgerlingen, Württemburg, Germany, c. sixth century BCE.
The prehistoric Celtic Horned Lord, Cernunnos, exhibits contained power and presence worthy of awe and veneration.

... a ritual phallus
... an initiation into the secrets of the earth
... that fearful tree of my childhood dream
... revealed as "the breath of life," the creative impulse.[10]

It was in line with the powerful phallic deities of the Celtic, German, Greek, Egyptian, and Middle and Far Eastern peoples, gods that are the embodiment of creative life-bestowing power. Much of Jung's lifework was to spring from these primitive and chthonic depths, emphasizing the maternal rather than the paternal principle.

What happened then was a kind of burial in the earth, and many years were to pass before I came out again. Today I know that it happened in order to bring the greatest possible amount of light into the darkness. It was an initiation into the realm of darkness. My intellectual life had its unconscious beginnings at that time.[11]

Outer life in the form of school shaped him further, adding to the gap between what the child was and what he tried to be to fit in with society. Jung designated his outer adapting personality as No. 1, his essential inner nature as No. 2. This interplay of opposites is played out in every individual to some degree, and in Jung to a more marked and conscious extent. Alone, he could sit contentedly on a stone and contemplate in wonder whether it was he or he was it. Or he could light fires with his schoolfriends

Wooden mannikin, carved by Jung.
Late in life, Jung created this depiction of the triple-aspected human being as body, feeling, and head, integrated through the repeated encircling arms.

Waning Moon #2; painting by Morris Graves, 1943.
As a child, Jung felt himself to be two distinct personalities: one outward and socially adapted, the other inward and essentially true.

and feel the flames were of secret significance. But, increasingly, the contact with his country playmates produced other effects.

> I found that they alienated me from myself. When I was with them I became different from the way I was at home. I joined in their pranks, or invented ones which at home would never have occurred to me, so it seemed; although, as I knew only too well, I could hatch up all sorts of things when I was alone. It seemed to me that the change in myself was due to the influence of my schoolfellows, who somehow misled me or compelled me to be different from what I thought I was. The influence of this wider world, this world which contained others besides my parents, seemed to me dubious if not altogether suspect and, in some obscure way, hostile…. It was as if I sensed a splitting of myself, and feared it. My inner security was threatened.[12]

Instinctively, without knowing why, he counteracted the threat of society to his inner self. Secretly, he carved a little wooden mannikin about two inches long, inked him black, made him a wool coat, and put him in a pencil box prepared as a bed. He added a smooth, oblong, blackish stone which he painted into an upper and lower

African mask,
Punu people, Gabon,
nineteenth century.
A deep calm seems
to emanate from the
mask's nine-scaled
central eye, which is
also a flowering tree.

half in the manner of a "soulstone," and which was also himself.

With great satisfaction, he then hid it high in the attic.

> No one could discover my secret and destroy it. I felt safe, and the tormenting sense of being at odds with myself was gone.... This possession of a secret had a very powerful formative effect on my character.... The little wooden figure with the stone was a first attempt, still unconscious and childish, to give shape to the secret. I was always absorbed by it and had the feeling I ought to fathom it; and yet I did not know what it was I was trying to express.[13]

The soulstone episode he later found to be akin to the traditions of ancient peoples like the Australian Aborigines and indigenous Africans.

That was, he said, the "climax and close" of his childhood with its prevailing sense of the "eternal."

ADOLESCENCE

In 1886, eleven-year-old Carl was enrolled in a secondary school in Basel. In less protected and wealthier surroundings, he became aware of his financial poverty, bringing on "a horrible secret envy."

The day-to-day routine world of education was background to a seesawing of diverging parts of his nature. At school his personality could be both sensitive to criticism and tactless to others, timidly self-effacing and fearlessly self-defensive with bullies, inwardly insecure and outwardly of superior confidence – the compensating swings of polarities not held in balance. Add to that oddish, not particularly popular, brilliant when interested but refusing to compete – a "troublemaker" to some.

A feeling of being an "outsider" set in. Boredom with school and an accidental fall propelled him into a neurotic illness that let him stay home and solitary. In falling, the thought had flashed excusingly in his mind, "Now you won't have to go to school any more." Out of that experience he first discovered what a neurosis was. He stayed in it for half a year. Then his conscience, upon overhearing his father's worried fear that the boy might be epileptic and unable to support himself, pushed him to the realization, "Why, then, I must get to work," and into diligent study.

In his imagination, Jung was two people at once – a powerful old man of the eighteenth century and also the poor twentieth-century schoolboy with holes in his socks who got good marks in most subjects but hated gymnastics, could draw only when inspired, and found mathematics "a torture."

The algebraic proposition that "A=B" struck him as "a downright lie or a fraud" to be equated with "sun=moon." His mind needed deeper explanations than formulas to allay his "moral doubts" about mathematics.

It was the same with religion when it was presented to him at a literal,

Teenaged Carl Jung, c. 1893.
Carl faces the camera with confidence.

dogmatic outer level. Divinity classes he found "unspeakably dull." "Lord Jesus" as taught remained an ambivalent figure, but the idea of God began to interest him, precisely because here was a mystery not easily fathomed, "a unique being of whom ... it was impossible to form any correct conception."

A decisive experience on the way home from school aged twelve initiated him into new uncharted depths.

The sky was gloriously blue, the day one of radiant sunshine. The roof of the cathedral glittered, the sun sparkling from the new, brightly glazed tiles. I was overwhelmed by the beauty of the sight, and thought: "The world is beautiful and the church is beautiful, and God made all this and sits above it far away in the blue sky on a golden throne and...." Here came a great hole in my thoughts, and a choking sensation. I felt numbed, and knew only, "Don't go on thinking now! Something terrible is coming, something I do not want to think, something I dare not even approach. Why not? Because I would be committing the most frightful of sins...."

On my long walk home ... I found my thoughts returning again and again to the beautiful cathedral which I loved so much, and to God sitting on the throne – and then my thoughts would fly off again as if they had received a powerful electric shock. I kept repeating to myself, "Don't think of it, just don't think of it!" I reached home in a pretty worked-up state....

That night I slept badly; again and again the forbidden thought, which I did not yet know, tried to break out, and I struggled desperately to fend it off. The next two days were sheer torture, and my mother was convinced I was ill....

On the third night, however, the torment became so unbearable that I no longer knew what to do. I awoke from a restless sleep just in time to catch myself thinking again about the cathedral and God. I had almost continued the thought! I felt my resistance weakening. Sweating with fear, I sat up in bed to shake off sleep. "Now it is coming; now it's serious! *I must think*. It must be thought out beforehand. *Why* should I think something I do not know? I don't want to, by God, that's sure. But *who* wants me to? Who wants to force me to think something I don't know and don't want to know? Where does this terrible will come from? ... I must find out what God wants with me, and

Invitation to the Soul; painting by Robert Taylor, 1996.
Jung's revelation showed him "God could be something terrible."

I must find out right away...." For I was now certain that He was the author of this desperate problem.... "Can it be that He wishes to test my obedience by imposing on me the unusual task of doing something against my own moral judgment and against the teachings of my religion, and even against His own commandment, something I am resisting with all my strength because I fear eternal damnation?" ... I thought it over again.... I gathered all my courage, as though I were about to leap forthwith into hell-fire, and let the thought come. I saw before me the cathedral, the blue sky. God sits on His golden throne, high above the world – and from under the throne an enormous turd falls upon the sparkling new roof, shatters it, and breaks the walls of the cathedral asunder.

So that was it! I felt an enormous, an indescribable relief. Instead of the expected damnation, grace had come upon me, and with it an unutterable bliss such as I had never known. I wept for happiness and gratitude. The wisdom and goodness of God had been revealed to me now that I had yielded to his inexorable command. It was as though I had experienced an illumination....

From that moment ... my true responsibility began. Why did God befoul His cathedral? That, for me, was a terrible thought. But then came the dim understanding that God could be something terrible. I had experienced a dark and terrible secret. It overshadowed my whole life....

It would never have occurred to me to speak of my experience openly, nor of my dream of the phallus in the underground temple, nor of my carved mannikin....

My entire youth can be understood in terms of this secret. It induced in me an almost unendurable loneliness.... Thus the pattern of my relationship to the world was already prefigured: today as then I am a solitary, because I know things and must hint at things which other people do not know, and usually do not even want to know.[14]

The old man, looking back, would say this experience had been "the guiding light" of his life. Teenage Carl still had to live with a personality which compensated for insecurity with an outer show of superior confidence. By fifteen he was given to violent rages, part of what he would later describe as his rather "bellicose" nature. In the midst of growing differentiation from his parents there could also be seen the generational legacy Jung was carrying into adulthood from them.

Both parents demonstrated the doubleness of being, the natural and adaptive, that can be particularly marked in tight, rigidly controlled, conventional societies. Outwardly Emilie Jung was a large, humorous, and kindly housewife, a good cook with conventional opinions and an undeveloped "literary gift," a "ready listener" and chatty talker combined. Underneath, a deeper, more powerful nature showed itself in sudden shifts to a penetrating observer whose utterances often influenced her son.

Emilie Preiswerk Jung.
Jung's identification with his mother caused him to see her too as having a dual nature: "By day she was a loving mother, but at night she seemed uncanny."

What she said on those occasions were so true and to the point that I trembled before it.... There was an enormous difference between my mother's two personalities.... By day she was a loving mother, but at night she seemed uncanny. Then she was like one of those seers who is at the same time a strange animal, like a priestess in a bear's cave. Archaic and ruthless; ruthless as truth and nature. At such moments she was the embodiment of what I have called the "natural mind."

I too have this archaic nature, and in me it is linked with the gift – not always pleasant – of seeing people and things as they are. I can let myself be deceived from here to Tipperary when I don't want to recognize something, and yet at bottom I know quite well how matters really stand.... This "insight" is based on instinct, or on a "*participation mystique*" with others.[15]

If mother and son were to some extent alike, they were close only to a point. Emilie treated young Carl "like a grownup," confiding in him things she couldn't tell her husband in their ambivalent married state. Even as a child, Jung withheld from her the "secret" life he didn't understand in himself, because "my confidence in her was strictly limited."

With adolescence, the dominance of parental relationship for Carl shifted from mother to father. At six he'd learned Latin from his linguistically gifted father and, during a time when his parents slept apart, he'd shared a bedroom with him. It was to this "dear and generous father" that Carl looked for mental communion and found instead his parent's unresolved complexities.

Paul Jung was a pastor of the Swiss Reformed Church Evangelical, a man quiet and unassuming in public and increasingly quarrelsome and bad-tempered in private. Along with the uneasy atmosphere generated by marital difficulties, his son felt a hollowness in his father's religious life which deeply disappointed his own lively questing. His father's religious instruction for Carl's confirmation "bored me to death." Belief without understanding seemed to be required.

> At that time, too, there arose in me profound doubts about everything my father said. When I heard him preaching about grace ... what he said sounded stale and hollow, like a tale told by someone who knows it only by hearsay and cannot quite believe it himself.... Later, when I was eighteen years old, I had many discussions with my father ... but [they] invariably came to an unsatisfactory end.... "Oh nonsense," he was in the habit of saying, "you always want to think. One ought not to think, but believe." I would think, "No, one must experience and know," but I would say, "Give me this belief," whereupon he would shrug and turn resignedly away.[16]

Lamentation of Orpheus; painting by Alexandre Séon, 1896.
The sensitive schoolboy felt cast ashore, alone with his inner muse. In contrast to his father's insistence on belief above all, Jung thought, "One must experience and know."

STUDIES

With no one to trust with his "secrets," teenage Carl's No. 2 personality – that of "God's world" and the "eternal" – began to fall into lonely isolation and No. 1 to take foreground. The now-studious Carl became an omnivorous reader of philosophy, had many clashes with his father, stopped going to church, and enrolled at the University of Basel, with the help of a grant, in 1895.

That was also the year an increasingly depressed Paul Jung was diagnosed with cancer, and died with Carl at his side. His father's death, as well as conferring on him responsibility as family manager, also liberated something else in his nineteen-year-old self. Later in life, Carl Jung was to call it the *persona*; the poet Yeats dubbed it the mask. To Jung's fellow students at university it was an astonishing change. The countrified bookworm suddenly joined in the swing of campus life and, as Albert Oeri recalled, came to be known as "the Barrel."

He seldom got drunk, but when he did he was loud. In the beginning he did not think much of Zofingia dances, idling about with the girls and such romantic stuff. But then he discovered that he was really quite a good dancer. At a large party in Zofingen ... he danced past and fell apparently hopelessly in love with a young French-speaking girl. The next morning he went into a shop, asked for two wedding rings, laid twenty centimes on the counter, said thank you very much, and was about to leave. But the owner stammered something about the rings costing so and so many francs. Then Jung gave them back, picked up his twenty centimes again and left the store, cursing the proprietor who had the nerve to keep him from getting engaged just because he happened to have no more than twenty centimes. The groom was very embarrassed, but he did not take up the subject again, and so "the Barrel" went on for quite a few more years without getting engaged.[17]

Jung described his student days as "intellectually alive" and "a time of friendships." With a directional push from his dream life he had elected to study medicine, adding on science, philosophy, archeology, and history. He said yes to Plato, Pythagoras, Heraclitus, Empedocles; no to the Aristotelian intellectualism of St. Thomas Aquinas and the Schoolmen. In Meister Eckhart he "felt a breath of life," somewhat fainter in Schopenhauer and Kant. Goethe's *Faust* was a distinct

Faust in His Study; etching by Rembrandt van Rijn, *c.* 1652.
"Two souls alas! Dwell in my breast!" Goethe, *Faust*, Part I.

influence, awakening in him the problem of opposites. Authorities like Zollner, Crookes, and "the seven volumes" of Swedenborg confirmed psychic phenomena as a new field meriting lifelong interest.

Avid reading told him the same psychic incidents were being reported in cultures worldwide – stories his country childhood had taken for granted: dreams foreseeing death, clocks stopping on its arrival, animals with a prior sense of storms and earthquakes, experiences of ghostly presences. Jung's own family history recounted generations of psychically sensitive individuals. Now, with Hélène Preiswerk, a young female relative, as medium, he investigated séances. At home, a solid table split unexplainedly; a knife in a drawer broke into four pieces.

Hélène Preiswerk.
Jung's cousin served as a medium in séances attended by the family. In a trance, she described a mandala, which Jung then drew.

All thought-provoking for Jung.

The observations of the spiritualists, weird and questionable as they seemed to me, were the first accounts I had seen of objective psychic phenomena.... For myself I found such possibilities extremely interesting and attractive. They added another dimension to my life; the world gained depth and background.[18]

The cost of that new interest was observed by fellow students.

"Jung will make a great storyteller yet," said one commentator with a laugh. But that was really what roused him to anger or even insults – when he was not taken seriously, not understood.[19]

I will not deny that Jung underwent a severe test of personal courage when he studied spiritualistic literature, did a good deal of experimentation in that field, and stood by his convictions unless they were modified by more psychological studies. He was up in arms when the official science of the day simply denied the existence of occult phenomena instead of investigating and trying to explain them.[20]

Jung's doctoral thesis was titled *On the Psychology and Pathology of So-Called Occult Phenomena* with his cousin Hélène as his research subject. Her abilities as a medium served as early pointers for Jung toward his discovery of the unconscious. Jung's autobiography details the twin pulls in him at that time:

What appealed to me in science were the concrete facts and their historical background, and in comparative religion the

Landscape; aquatint by Georges Rouault, 1938.
Between the poles of science and religion was psychiatry, "the place where the ... collision of nature and spirit became a reality."

spiritual problems, into which philosophy also entered. In science I missed the factor of meaning; and in religion, that of empiricism. Science met, to a very large extent, the needs of No. 1 personality, whereas the humane or historical studies provided beneficial instruction for No. 2.

Torn between these two poles, I was for a long time unable to settle on anything.[21]

What was he to specialize in professionally? How to reconcile diverse interests into one prime study? It was the opening pages of a book by Kraft Ebbing which had first pointed him unmistakably to the then despised arena of psychiatry.

My heart suddenly began to pound. I had to stand up and draw a deep breath. My excitement was intense, for it had become clear to me, in a flash of illumination, that for me the only possible goal was psychiatry. Here alone the two currents of my interest could flow together and in a united stream dig their own bed. Here was the empirical field common to biological and spiritual facts, which I had everywhere sought and nowhere found. Here at last was the place where the collision of nature and spirit became a reality.[22]

Reactions to his choice from teachers and fellow students was "amazement and disappointment." Once again he began to feel like an outsider, "the old wound ... began to ache again," but the years of study had grown enough confidence in him that he could add "but now I understand why."

FIRST WORK

At twenty-five Jung entered his "years of apprenticeship" at Burghölzli Hospital in Zürich as an assistant to its director. A rapid series of promotions elevated him to Deputy Director of the Hospital, and he also became a lecturer at the University of Zürich. His innovative work on *dementia praecox* (schizophrenia) and complexes attracted attention, especially in America, bringing in private patients.

From the outset the twenty-five-year-old assistant at Burghölzli Hospital related to patients and their psychic disorders in his own way. Unlike most practitioners of his day, he actually listened to their personal stories, paid attention to the context of their fantasies, discussed their dreams, and developed further a word-association method in the process.

> Dominating my interests and research was the burning question: "What actually takes place inside the mentally ill?" ... Psychiatry teachers were not interested in what the patient had to say, but rather in how to make a diagnosis or how to describe

Jung's diploma from the Burghölzli Clinic of the University of Zürich, 1900.
Jung said this helped guarantee him a normal existence in times of inner strife.

symptoms and to compile statistics. From the clinical point of view which then prevailed, the human personality of the patient, his individuality, did not matter at all…. Patients were labeled, rubber-stamped with a diagnosis and, for the most part, that settled the matter. The psychology of the mental patient played no role whatsoever.[23]

Through my work with the patients I realized that paranoid ideas and hallucinations contain a germ of meaning. A personality, a life history, a pattern of hopes and desires lie behind the psychosis. The fault is ours if we do not understand them…. At bottom we discover nothing new and unknown in the mentally ill; rather, we encounter the substratum of our own natures.[24]

I treat every patient as individually as possible, because the solution of the problem is always an individual one. Universal rules can be postulated only with a grain of salt. A psychological truth is valid only if it can be reversed. A solution which would be out of the question for me may be just the right one for someone else…. The crucial point is that I confront the patient as one human being to another.[25]

In therapy the problem is always the whole person, never the symptom alone. We must ask questions which challenge the whole personality.[26]

EMMA

In his autobiography Jung says that the strongest element in his nature was "a passionate urge toward understanding." His own basic psychology he defined as primarily intuitive and intellectual. An intuitive knowing that penetrated through the everyday observable realities was a marked feature of his life, professionally and personally. At age twenty-one, while making a social call, he glimpsed a fourteen-year-old schoolgirl in pigtails on the stairs. Like a flash it was clear to him: *This is my wife!*

> I was deeply shaken by this, for I had really only seen her for a brief instant, but I knew immediately with absolute certainty that she would be my wife.[27]

Six years later Emma Rauschenbach refused the young doctor's first proposal of

Wedding photograph of Carl and Emma Jung, 1903.
Emma was twenty-one and Jung was twenty-eight at the time of their wedding.

marriage, but said yes to the second. Their unpublished love letters have, according to one reader, "romantic beauty and sentimental charm." Their marriage, in 1903, produced four daughters and a son.

Emma, described as quiet, clever, and self-possessed, began to assist Jung professionally even early in their marriage. Her engaging manner and spontaneous gaiety were distinct assets socially. Her dowry, from a well-to-do manufacturing family, meant financial difficulty was past for Jung. Over the front door of the house they built in Küsnacht were carved, in Latin, the words of the Delphic Oracle: "Invoked or not invoked, the god will be present."

Jung's published letters to Emma are mostly about his professional travels – vivid impressions of people, places, and nature, eloquent and humorous. This from the steamer *Kaiser Wilhelm der Grosse* on a stormy Atlantic crossing:

> Outside from time to time a wave thundered against the ship. The objects in my cabin had all come to life: the sofa cushion crawled about on the floor in the semi-darkness; a recumbent shoe sat up, looked around in astonishment, and then shuffled quietly off under the sofa; a standing shoe turned wearily on its side and followed its mate. Now the scene changed. I realized that the shoes had gone under the sofa to fetch my bag and briefcase. The whole company paraded over to join the big trunk under the bed. One sleeve of my shirt on the sofa waved longingly after them, and from inside the chests and drawers came rumbles and rattles. Suddenly there was a terrible crash under my floor, a rattling, clattering and tinkling. One of the kitchens is underneath me. There, at one blow, five hundred plates had been awakened from their deathlike torpor and with a single bold leap had put a sudden end to their dreary existence as slaves. In all the cabins round about, unspeakable groans betrayed the secrets of the menu. I slept like a top, and this morning the wind is beginning to blow from another side....
>
> What has man to say here, especially at night when the ocean is alone with the starry sky? One looks out silently, surrendering all self-importance, and many old sayings and images scurry through the mind; a low voice says something about the age-oldness and infinitude of the "far-swelling murmurous sea," of "the waves of the sea and of love," of Leukothea, the lovely goddess who appears in the foam of the seething waves to travel-weary Odysseus and gives him the pearly veil which saves him

from Poseidon's storm. The sea is like music; it has all the dreams of the soul within itself and sounds them over. The beauty and grandeur of the sea consists in our being forced down into the fruitful bottomlands of our own psyches, where we confront and re-create ourselves....[28]

Front door of Jung's house in Küsnacht, Switzerland.
Over the front door is written, "*Vocatus atque non vocatus deus aderit.*" ("Invoked or not invoked, the god will be present.")

JUNG AND FREUD

Jung at that stage was returning from a visit to America with Sigmund Freud, whom he described as "the first man of real importance" in his life. It was 1909, the year after the First International Psychoanalytic Congress in Salzburg. Both had been invited to speak in Massachusetts, and both had been appointed honorary Doctors of Law at Clark University. He wrote to his wife,

> Now I may place an L.L.D. after my name. Impressive, what? …
> Freud is in seventh heaven, and I am glad with all my heart to
> see him so.[29]

Jung, a successful senior physician, author, and lecturer in Switzerland, had publicly supported the pioneering Freud in years when it was damaging academically to do so.

Freud, "in splendid isolation," had founded the psychoanalytic movement near the turn of the century in Vienna. It was his 1905 findings on the sexual instinct in childhood that brought "the maximum of odium" on Freud's name.

World conference of psychologists, Clark University, Worcester, Massachusetts, 1909. Jung (front row, third from right) lectured on a word-association experiment. Sigmund Freud, on Jung's right, described the psychoanalytic method. Both men received honorary doctorates from Clark University.

In the early 1900s Jung read Freud's groundbreaking book *The Interpretation of Dreams* and "discovered how it all linked up with my own ideas." He began to cite Freud's writings in his work. A correspondence began in 1906 after Jung sent Freud a publication of his own. Yet even in the first letter from Jung, a major difference between them was foreshadowed.

[It] seems to me that though the genesis of hysteria is predominantly, it is not exclusively, sexual. I take the same view of your sexual theory.[30]

Dear Colleague,
Your writings have long led me to suspect that your appreciation of my psychology does not extend to all my views on hysteria and the problem of sexuality, but I venture to hope that in the course of the years you will come much closer to me than you now think possible....
Yours very sincerely,
Dr. Freud[31]

Jung's book on schizophrenia was published the following year, the introduction acknowledging "how much I am indebted to the brilliant discoveries of Freud," while stressing "one can very well maintain an independent judgment." It led to the two men meeting for the first time at Freud's home in Vienna.

We met at one o'clock in the afternoon and talked virtually without a pause for thirteen hours. Freud was the first man of real importance I had encountered; in my experience up to that time, no one else could compare with him. There was nothing the least trivial in his attitude. I found him extremely intelligent, shrewd, and altogether remarkable. And yet my first impressions of him remained somewhat tangled; I could not make him out.

What he said about his sexual theory impressed me. Nevertheless his words could not remove my hesitations and doubts. I tried to advance these reservations of mine on several occasions, but each time he would attribute them to my lack of experience. Freud was right; in those days I had not enough experience to support my objections....

Above all, Freud's attitude toward the spirit seemed to me highly questionable. Wherever, in a person or in a work of

Sun and Moon Battle; manuscript illumination from *Aurora consurgens*, late fifteenth century.

The relationship between Freud and Jung was a meeting of opposites – complementary at first, becoming antagonistic in time.

art, an expression of spirituality came to light, he suspected it and insinuated that it was repressed sexuality. Anything that could not be directly interpreted as sexuality he referred to as "psychosexuality." I protested.... Culture would then appear as a mere farce, the morbid consequence of repressed sexuality. "Yes," he assented, "so it is, and that is just a curse of fate against which we are powerless to contend." I was by no means disposed to agree, or to let it go at that, but still I did not feel competent to argue it out with him.[32]

Freud came to regard Jung as his son and heir. For Jung, Freud was a father figure, though only for a time. Nineteen years separated the two – and, increasingly, a clash of ideas.

Mostly they met by letter. Their voluminous correspondence over seven years was an intimate discussion of scientific ideas, patients, colleagues, the struggles of the psychiatric movement, their personal lives, and their own relationship. It was a correspondence Jung didn't want published until thirty years after his death. At eighty-three he called it "an unfortunately inexpungeable reminder of the incredible folly that filled the days of my youth." In it is revealed many aspects of his personality and growth at a time when few other letters have been preserved.

Jung, at an early stage, confided to Freud that a traumatic boyhood experience with a close family friend, a middle-aged man, was influencing emotional overtones of his relationship to him.[33]

> Your last two letters contain references to my laziness in writing…. Actually – and I confess this to you with a struggle … my veneration for you has something of the character of a "religious" crush. Though it does not really bother me, I still feel it is disgusting and ridiculous because of its undeniable erotic undertone. This abominable feeling comes from the fact that as a boy I was the victim of a sexual assault by a man I once worshipped….
>
> This feeling, which I still have not got rid of, hampers me considerably.[34]

> Dear Professor Freud,
> Heartiest thanks for your letter, which worked wonders for me. You are absolutely right to extol humor as the only decent reaction to the inevitable. This was also my principle until the repressed material got the better of me, luckily only at odd moments.[35]

Intellectual stimulus, excitement of discovery, mutual enjoyment – nothing was held back. Jung's high temper could be seen when he sided with Freud on a dressing-down delivered by the latter to a vitriolic critic of psychoanalysis.

> Dear Professor Freud,
> The adventure with "Schöttlander" is marvelous; of course the slimy bastard was lying. I hope you roasted, flayed, and impaled the fellow with such genial ferocity that he got a lasting taste for once of the effectiveness of psychoanalysis. I subscribe to your final judgment with all my heart. Such is the nature of these beasts. Since I could read the filth in him from his face I would have gone for his throat. I hope to God you told him all the truths so plainly that even his hen's brain could absorb them…. Had I been in your shoes I would have softened up his guttersnipe complex with a sound Swiss thrashing.[36]

Jung, in a photograph taken about the time he began his seven-year correspondence with the founder of the psychoanalytic movement, Sigmund Freud.

In late 1908 the imminent birth of Jung's only son, Franz, brought a charming series of family vignettes beginning with a solicitous enquiry from Freud.

Dear friend,
No, the dawn is not yet. We must carefully tend our little lamp, for the night will be long.... In the meantime, I venture to hope, fate has made you a father again.... Let me hear from you; until then I assume that the valiant mother is well; to her husband she must indeed be more precious than all her children, just as the method must be valued more highly than the results obtained by it.[37]

Dear Professor Freud,

Heartiest thanks for your congratulatory telegram! You can imagine our joy. The birth went off normally, mother and child are doing well.[38]

Contributions by my four-year-old Agathli: the evening before Fränzli's birth I asked her what she would say if the stork brought her a little brother? "Then I shall kill it," she said quick as lightning with an embarrassed, sly expression, and would not let herself be pinned down to this theme. The baby was born during the night. Early next morning I carried her to my wife's bedside; she was tense and gazed in alarm at the rather wan-looking mother, without showing any joy; found nothing to say about the situation. The same morning, when Mama was alone, the little one suddenly ran to her, flung her arms round her neck and asked anxiously: "But, Mama, you don't have to die, do you...?"

Finally, on my advice, my wife enlightened A.... (Children grow in the mother like flowers on plants.) Next day I was in bed with influenza. A. came in with a shy, rather startled look on her face, wouldn't approach the bed but asked: "Have you a plant in your tummy too?" Ran off merry and carefree when this possibility was ruled out.[39]

What an enchantment such a child is! Only recently A. praised the beauty of her little brother to her grandmother: "And look what a pretty little boy's bottom he has."[40]

My Agathli continues merrily with her discoveries. New and delightful attempts at explanation have resulted. The act of birth is now fully understood, as the little one announced in an amusing game. She stuck her doll between her legs under her skirt so that only the head was showing, and cried: "Look, a baby is coming!" Then, pulling it out slowly: "And now it's all out." Only the role of the father is still obscure and a subject for dreams.[41]

We simply listen and meddle as little as possible. A great outcry this morning: Mama must come – I want to go into your room –

Adam and Little Eve; painting by Paul Klee, 1921.

The facts of life, as discovered by four-year-old Agathli, were passed on by her father to Freud.

What is Papa doing? – But Mama won't have her in the room.... Later, when we had got up, Agathli hops in, jumps into my bed, lies flat on her stomach, flails and kicks out with her legs like a horse – "Is that what Papa does? That's what Papa does, isn't it?" ... My colleagues are encouraging me to write the thing up for the *Jahrbuch*.[42]

Freud was the more demanding correspondent of the two, sending off an anxious telegram if an expected letter was delayed. In 1909 Jung, "under a terrific strain," excused a tardy reply, confiding several problems, especially one involving an ex-patient, Sabina Spielrein.

The last and worst straw is that a complex is playing Old Harry with me: a woman patient, whom years ago I pulled out of a very sticky neurosis with unstinting effort, has violated my confidence and my friendship in the most mortifying way imaginable. She has kicked up a vile scandal solely because I denied myself the pleasure of giving her a child. I have always acted the gentleman toward her, but before the bar of my rather too sensitive conscience I nevertheless don't feel clean, and that is what hurts the most because my intentions were always honorable. But you know how it is – the devil can use even the best of things for the fabrication of filth. Meanwhile I have learnt an unspeakable amount of marital wisdom, for until now I had a totally inadequate idea of my polygamous components despite all self-analysis. Now I know where and how the devil can be laid by the heels. These painful yet extremely salutary insights have churned me up hellishly inside, but for that very reason, I hope, have secured me moral qualities which will be of the greatest advantage to me in later life. The relationship with my wife has gained enormously in assurance and depth.[43]

The woman in question had been discussed between them in earlier years without being named, referred to as a "hysterical patient" who "admits that actually her greatest wish is to have a child by me who would fulfill her unfillable wishes."

It was classic transference, a projection by the patient onto the doctor, and in this case, too, a lurking transference by doctor onto patient, a difficult point in psychiatric interaction in which the doctor also surfaces little-aired aspects of his psyche. Neither had been fully resolved by the end of treatment, or in subsequent brinkmanship relatedness between them over the following years,

until I saw that an unintended wheel had started turning, whereupon I finally broke with her. She was, of course, systematically planning my seduction, which I considered inopportune. Now she is seeking revenge.[44]

Rumor, and a letter from Spielrein, had already reached Freud, who advised from a longer experience of life:

Dear friend,
Such experiences, though painful, are necessary and hard to avoid. Without them we cannot really know life and what we are dealing with. I myself have never been taken in quite so badly, but I have come very close to it a number of times and had *a narrow escape*.

I believe that only grim necessities weighing on my work, and the fact that I was ten years older than yourself when I came to psychoanalysis, have saved me from similar experiences. But no lasting harm is done. They help us to develop the thick skin we need and to dominate "countertransference," which is after all a permanent problem for us....

The way these women manage to charm us with every conceivable psychic perfection until they have attained their purpose is one of nature's greatest spectacles. Once that has been done or the contrary has become a certainty, the constellation changes amazingly.

Sincerely yours,

Freud[45]

Further letters from Spielrein involved Freud, bringing more fatherly advice: "don't go too far in the direction of contrition and reaction." Days later the situation peaked, drawing a full unburdening from Jung.

I have good news to report of my Spielrein affair. I took too black a view of things.... The day before yesterday she turned up at my house and had a *very decent* talk with me ... she has freed herself from the transference in the best and nicest way and has suffered no relapse.... Although not succumbing to helpless remorse, I nevertheless deplore the sins I have committed, for I am largely to blame for the high-flying hopes of my former patient.... I discussed with her the problem of the child, imagining that I was talking theoretically, but naturally Eros was lurking in the background. Thus I imputed all the other wishes and hopes entirely to my patient without seeing the same thing in myself. When the situation had become so tense that the continued perseveration of the relationship could be rounded out only by sexual acts, I defended myself in a manner that cannot be justified morally. Caught in my delusion that I was the victim of the sexual wiles of my patient, I wrote to her mother that I was not the gratifier of her daughter's sexual desires but merely her doctor, and that she should free me from her. In view of the fact that the patient had shortly before been my friend and enjoyed my full confidence, my action was a piece of knavery which I very reluctantly confess to you as my father.[46]

Sigmund Freud, 1938 (the year before his death).
Freud saw himself as a father figure to Jung. According to the Oedipus myth, the son must slay his father. To Freud, this described sexual jealousy; to Jung, the myth was a metaphor for the new growing from the old.

But the role of son was already in shift. 1909 saw the peak year of the Freud/Jung relationship – and its turning point. In the spring the two men had their third domestic meeting when Jung and Emma stayed with the Freuds for five days. Jung's autobiographical account of the visit records the emergence of differences in their attitudes to psychic phenomena on the last evening.

It interested me to hear Freud's views on precognition and on parapsychology in general. When I visited him in Vienna in 1909 I asked him what he thought of these matters. Because of his materialistic prejudice, he rejected this entire complex of questions as nonsensical, and did so in terms of so shallow a positivism that I had difficulty in checking the sharp retort on the tip of my tongue. It was some years before he recognized the seriousness of parapsychology and acknowledged the factuality of "occult" phenomena.

While Freud was going on this way, I had a curious sensation. It was as if my diaphragm were made of iron and were becoming red-hot – a glowing vault. And at that moment there was such a loud report in the bookcase, which stood right next to us, that we both started up in alarm, fearing the thing was going to topple over on us. I said to Freud: "There, that is an example of a so-called catalytic exteriorization phenomenon."

"Oh, come," he exclaimed. "That is sheer bosh."

"It is not," I replied. "You are mistaken, Herr Professor. And to prove my point I now predict that in a moment there will be another loud report!" Sure enough, no sooner had I said the words than the same detonation went off in the bookcase.

To this day I do not know what gave me this certainty. But I knew beyond all doubt that the report would come again. Freud only stared aghast at me ... this incident aroused his mistrust of me, and I had the feeling I had done something against him.[47]

From Küsnacht the debate continued, Jung's statement that the final part of the visit "has ... freed me inwardly from the oppressive sense of your paternal authority" provoking this letter from Freud:

Dear friend,

It is strange that on the very same evening when I formally adopted you as eldest son and anointed you ... as my successor and crown prince, you should have divested me of my paternal dignity, which divesting seems to have given you as much pleasure as I, on the contrary, derived from the investiture of your person. Now I am afraid of falling back into the father role with you if I tell you how I feel about the poltergeist business. But I must, because my attitude is not what you might otherwise think. I don't deny that your stories and your experiment made a deep impression on me.... At first I was inclined to accept ... as proof, if the sound that was so frequent while you were here were not heard again after your departure – but since then I have heard it repeatedly, not, however, in connection with my thoughts and never when I am thinking about you or this particular problem of yours.... My credulity, or at least my willingness to believe, vanished with the magic of your personal presence; once again, for some inward reasons I can't put my finger on, it strikes me as quite unlikely that such phenomena should exist.... Accordingly, I put my fatherly horn-rimmed spectacles on again and warn my dear son to keep a cool head, for it is better not to understand something than make such great sacrifices to understanding....

Consequently, I shall receive further news of your investigations of the spook complex with the interest one accords to a charming delusion in which one does not oneself participate. Yours, Freud[48]

But psychic phenomena was not the only subject of disagreement between them that last evening.

I can still recall vividly how Freud said to me, "My dear Jung, promise me never to abandon the sexual theory. That is the most essential thing of all. You see, we must make a dogma of it, an unshakable bulwark." ... In some astonishment I asked him, "A bulwark – against what?" To which he replied, "Against the black tide of mud" – and here he hesitated for a moment, then added – "of occultism." ... It was the words "bulwark" and "dogma" that alarmed me ... that no longer has anything to do with scientific judgment; only with a personal power drive.

This was the thing that struck at the heart of our friendship. I knew that I would never be able to accept such an attitude. What Freud seemed to mean by "occultism" was virtually everything that philosophy and religion, including the rising contemporary science of parapsychology, had learned about the psyche.[49]

Six months later came the American trip with its honors to both men and the first of two fainting episodes by Freud in Jung's presence, prompted by anxiety about presumed "death wishes" to the father. The voyage dealt another blow to the relationship.

We were together every day, and analyzed each other's dreams. At the time I had a number of important ones, but Freud could make nothing of them. I did not regard that as any reflection upon him, for it sometimes happens to the best analyst that he is unable to unlock the riddle of a dream. It was a human failure, and I would never have wanted to discontinue our dream analyses on that account. On the contrary, they meant a great deal to me, and I found our relationship exceedingly valuable. I regarded Freud as an older, more mature and experienced personality, and felt like a son in that respect. But then something happened which proved to be a severe blow to the whole relationship.

Freud had a dream – I would not think it right to air the problem it involved. I interpreted it as best I could, but added that a great deal more could be said about it if he would supply me with some additional details from his private life. Freud's response to these words was a curious look – a look of the utmost suspicion. Then he said, "But I cannot risk my authority!" At that moment he lost it altogether. That sentence burned itself into my memory; and in it the end of our relationship was already foreshadowed. Freud was placing personal authority above truth.[50]

Two streams were now operating in Jung. Inwardly, a number of puzzling symbolic dreams were taking him deeper into the psyche, past the personal to what he later called the collective level of the unconscious. The result was a plunge into new studies – mythology, archeology, the Christian Gnostics, primitive cultures,

Painting of Emma Jung, printed in a local Swiss newspaper.

Mrs. Jung sought to diffuse the growing antipathies between her husband and his mentor by writing to Freud.

astrology – and the beginnings of what was to be a fateful book, setting out thinking divergent from that of Freud.

Concurrently the successful professional man now acquired more honors, with Freud's approval, when the International Psychoanalytic Association was founded with Jung as president and editor of its scientific journal. An honorary doctorate followed a series of lectures in New York, and Part One of *Transformations and Symbols of the Libido* was published.

It was Emma Jung who signaled the undertones of the Freud/Jung relationship after a four-day visit by Freud to the Jung family home. Unknown to her husband she wrote to Freud.

Dear Professor Freud,
I don't really know how I am summoning the courage to write you this letter....

Since your visit I have been tormented by the idea that your relation with my husband is not altogether as it should be, and since it definitely ought not to be like this I want to try to do whatever is in my power. I do not know whether I am deceiving myself when I think you are somehow not quite in agreement with *Transformations of Libido*. You didn't speak of it at all and yet I think it would do you both so much good if you got down to a thorough discussion of it. Or is it something else? If so, please tell me what, dear Herr Professor; for I cannot bear to see you so resigned and I even believe that your resignation relates not only to your real children … but also to your spiritual sons; otherwise you would have so little need to be resigned.[51]

Dear Professor Freud,
You may imagine how overjoyed and honored I am by the confidence you have in Carl, but it almost seems to me as though you were sometimes giving too much – do you not see in him the follower and fulfiller more than you need? Doesn't one often give much because one wants to keep much?

Why are you thinking of giving up already instead of enjoying your well-earned fame and success…?

No, you should rejoice and drink to the full the happiness of victory after having struggled for so long. And do not think of Carl with a father's feeling: "He will grow, but I must dwindle," but rather as one human being thinks of another, who like you has his own law to fulfill.

Don't be angry with me.

With warm love and veneration, Emma Jung[52]

The final letter in that series throws light on the dynamics of the Jung marital relationship, which had its own difficulties.

My Dear Professor Freud,

Heartfelt thanks for your letter. Please don't worry, I am not always as despondent as I was in my last letter.... Usually I am quite at one with my fate and see very well how lucky I am, but from time to time I am tormented by the conflict about how I can hold my own against Carl. I find I have no friends, all the people who associate with us really only want to see Carl, except for a few boring and to me quite uninteresting persons.

Naturally the women are all in love with him, and with the men I am instantly cordoned off as the wife of the father or friend. Yet I have a strong need for people and Carl too says I should stop concentrating on him and the children, but what on earth am I to do? What with my strong tendency to autoerotism it is very difficult ... because I can never compete with Carl. In order to emphasize this I usually have to talk extra stupidly when in company....

You will now understand why I felt so bad at the thought that I had lost your favor, and I was also afraid Carl might notice something. At any rate he now knows about the exchange of letters, as he was astonished to see one of your letters addressed to me; but I have revealed only a little of their content.[53]

A life-changing decision was looming for Jung. What was he to do with his research into Part Two of his *Transformations* book? His understanding of it revealed facets of the libido concept and incest taboos that diverged completely from Freud.

Their correspondence records a mounting crisis.

Dear Professor Freud,

On the question of incest, I am grieved to see what powerful affects you have mobilized for your counter-offensive against my suggestions. Since I think I have objective reasons on my side, I am forced to stand by my interpretation of the incest concept, and see no way out of the dilemma. It is not for frivolous reasons or from regressive prejudices that I have been led to this formulation, as will, I hope, become clear to you when you read my painstaking and intricate examination of the whole problem in my second part.... I set out with the idea of corroborating the old view of incest, but was obliged to see that things are different from what I expected....

I hope we shall be able to come to an understanding on controversial points later on. It seems I shall have to go my own way for some time to come. But you know how obstinate we Swiss are.
With kind regards, Jung[54]

Dear friend,
About the libido question, we shall see. The nature of the change you have made is not quite clear to me and I know nothing of its motivation. Once I am better informed, I shall surely be able to switch to objectivity, precisely because I am well aware of my bias. Even if we cannot come to terms immediately, there is no reason to suppose that this scientific difference will detract from our personal relations. I can recall that there were profounder differences between us at the beginning of our relationship.
Yours, Freud[55]

Dear Professor Freud,
With me it is not a question of caprice but of fighting for what I hold to be true. In this matter no personal regard for you can restrain me.... Obviously I would prefer to be on personal terms with you, to whom I owe so much, but I want your objective judgment and no feelings of resentment. I think I deserve this much if only for reasons of expediency: I have done more to promote the psychoanalytic movement than Rank, Stekel, Adler, etc. put together. I can only assure you that there is no resistance on my side, unless it be my refusal to be treated like a fool riddled with complexes.
Most sincerely, Jung[56]

Dear Dr. Jung,
I am gradually coming to terms with this [libido] paper ... and

Isis and Osiris; vignette from the *Papyrus of Ani/ The Egyptian Book of the Dead*, Egypt, c. 1500 BCE. Osiris and Isis, the archetypal loving couple, were brother and sister as well as husband and wife. Osiris (Will) was dismembered by his brother Seth (Darkness). Isis (Wisdom) gathered the scattered pieces of his body and returned him to life. Egyptian rulers were encouraged to wed siblings in emulation of the gods. Freud and Jung disputed the questions of incest and mysticism; this was the source of their ultimate break.

I now believe that in it you have brought us a great revelation, though not the one you intended. You seem to have solved the riddle of all mysticism, showing it to be based on the symbolic utilization of complexes that have outlived their function.
With regards to you and your wife,
Your untransformed Freud[57]

Dear Professor Freud,
As evidence that you – if I may be permitted so disrespectful an expression – *underestimate* my work by a very wide margin, I would cite your remark that "without intending it, I have solved

the riddle of all mysticism, showing it to be based on the symbolic utilization of complexes that have outlived their function."

My dear Professor, forgive me again, but this sentence shows me that you deprive yourself of the possibility of understanding my work by your underestimation of it. You speak of this insight as though it were some kind of pinnacle, whereas actually it is at the very bottom of the mountain. This insight has been self-evident to us for years. Again, please excuse my frankness. It is only occasionally that I am afflicted with the purely human desire to be understood *intellectually* and not be measured by the yardstick of neurosis.
With kind regards,
Jung[58]

Dear Dr. Jung,
The habit of taking objective statements personally is not only a (regressive) human trait, but also a very specific Viennese failing. I shall be very glad if such claims are not made on you. But are you "objective" enough to consider [your] following slip without anger?

"Even Adler's cronies do not regard me as one of *yours*."
Yours nevertheless, Freud[59]

Dear Professor Freud,
May I say a few words to you in earnest? ... your technique of treating your pupils like patients is a *blunder*.... You go around sniffing out all the symptomatic actions in your vicinity, thus reducing everyone to the level of sons and daughters who blushingly admit the existence of their faults. Meanwhile you remain on top as the father, sitting pretty....

You see, my dear Professor, so long as you hand out this stuff I don't give a damn for my symptomatic actions; they shrink to nothing in comparison with the formidable beam in my brother Freud's eye. I am not in the least neurotic – touch wood! I have submitted ... to analysis and am much the better for it. You know, of course, how far a patient gets with self-analysis: *not* out of his neurosis – just like you. If ever you should rid yourself entirely of your complexes and stop playing the father to your sons and instead of aiming continually at their weak spots take a good look at your own for a change, then I will mend my ways and at one stroke uproot the vice of being in two minds about you....

No doubt you will be outraged by this peculiar token of friendship, but it may do you good all the same.
With best regards,
Most sincerely yours, Jung[60]

3.1.1913
Dear Mr. President,
Dear Doctor,
Your allegation that I treat my followers like patients is demonstrably untrue. In Vienna I am reproached for the exact opposite....

Otherwise your letter cannot be answered. It creates a situation that would be difficult to deal with in a personal talk and totally impossible in correspondence. It is a convention among us analysts that none of us needs feel ashamed of his own bit of neurosis. But one who while behaving abnormally keeps shouting that he is normal gives ground for the suspicion that he lacks insight into his illness. Accordingly, I propose that we abandon our personal relations entirely.[61]

Photograph by Peter Angelo Simon, 1997.
By 1913, Jung and Freud had stopped speaking to each other.

DESCENT

After the break with Freud, all my friends and acquaintances dropped away. My book was declared to be rubbish; I was a mystic, and that settled the matter. Riklin and Maeder alone stuck by me. But I had foreseen my isolation and harbored no illusion about the reactions of my so-called friends. I realized that the chapter "The Sacrifice" meant my own sacrifice.[62]

In more ways than one, Jung said he lived most of his adult life until nearly forty on personality No. 1 – ambition, career, success, family, international repute. Now only family and private practice remained. He resigned his public posts including those with the Psychoanalytic Society. His old intellectual life drew to a standstill as he found himself incapable of reading a scientific book. For the next six years his inner personality asserted itself in earnest, drawing him deeper and deeper into the unconscious of his own psyche.

After the parting of the ways with Freud, a period of inner uncertainty began for me. It would be no exaggeration to call it a state of disorientation. I felt totally suspended in mid-air, for I had not yet found my own footing....

I lived as if under constant inner pressure. At times this became so strong that I suspected there was some psychic disturbance in myself.... Retrospection led to nothing but a fresh acknowledgment of my own ignorance.... I said to myself, "Since I know nothing at all, I shall simply do whatever occurs to me...."

The first thing that came to the surface was a childhood memory from perhaps my tenth or eleventh year. At that time I had had a spell of playing passionately with building blocks. I distinctly recalled how I had built little houses and castles.... To my astonishment, this memory was accompanied by a good deal of emotion. "Aha," I said to myself, "there is still life in these things. The small boy is still around, and possesses a creative life which I lack. But how can I make my way to it?" ... I had no choice but to return to it and take up once more that child's life with his childish games. This moment was a turning point in my fate, but I gave in only after endless resistances and with a sense

Photograph by Peter Angelo Simon, 1997.
"After the parting of the ways with Freud, a period of inner uncertainty began for me. It would be no exaggeration to call it a state of disorientation. I felt totally suspended in mid-air, for I had not yet found my own footing...."

of resignation. For it was a painfully humiliating experience to realize there was nothing to be done except play childish games.

Nevertheless I began accumulating suitable stones.... And I started building: cottages, a castle, a whole village ... the church ... an altar ... every day ... as soon as I was through eating, I began playing, and continued to do so until the patients arrived.... It released a stream of fantasies which I later carefully wrote down.[63]

What Jung called his confrontation with the unconscious has been known to humanity from spiritual history through the aeons. It's in the Gnostic texts of early Christianity, the dark night of the soul of St. John of the Cross, the shamanic trials of primal cultures, the Nekyia episode of Homer's *Odyssey*, the night sea journey recorded in many mythologies. It is personal and collective, an initiation of death and rebirth, only undertaken by the few and always perilous.

For Jung his inner experience and the life of his time coincided. Descent also brought repeated visions of European catastrophe in rivers of blood, and a warning – the year was 1913.

An inner voice told him:

"Look at it well; it is wholly real and it will be so. You cannot doubt it."

I drew the conclusion that they had to do with me myself, and decided that I was menaced by a psychosis. The idea of war did not occur to me at all.[64]

An incessant stream of fantasies had been released.... I felt as if gigantic blocks of stone were tumbling down upon me. One thunderstorm followed another.... When I endured these assaults of the unconscious I had an unswerving conviction that I was obeying a higher will.... I knew that I had to let myself plummet down into them.... I felt not only violent resistance to this, but a distinct fear. For I was afraid of losing command of myself and becoming a prey to the fantasies – and as a psychiatrist I realized only too well what that meant....

I resolved upon the decisive step. I was sitting at my desk once more, thinking over my fears. Then I let myself drop. Suddenly it was as though the ground literally gave way beneath my feet, and I plunged down into dark depths. I could not fend off a feeling of panic.[65]

Visions, dreams, and inner voices pounded his consciousness along with a sense of their meaning.

a dark cave ... a dwarf with a leathery skin ... glowing red crystal ... running water ... a corpse floated by ... a gigantic black scarab ... a red, newborn sun ... blood. A thick jet of it.

Shadow Cornered; painting by C.G. Jung.
Jung depicted his sense of despair and isolation in a painting from *The Red Book.*

I was stunned by this vision ... a drama of death and renewal. Six days later, I had the following dream.

I ... with an unknown brownskinned man ... in a lonely, rocky mountain landscape ... Siegfried's horn ... we had to kill him ... Siegfried ... on a chariot made of the bones of the dead ... at furious speed ... we shot at him ... struck dead ... a tremendous downfall of rain ... an unbearable feeling of guilt....

I tried ... to fall asleep again, but a voice within me said, "*You must understand the dream, and must do so at once! ... If you do not understand the dream, you must shoot yourself!*"

Suddenly the meaning of the dream dawned on me ... a sign of my secret identity with Siegfried, as well as of the grief a man feels when he is forced to sacrifice his ideal and his conscious attitudes ... for there are higher things than the ego's will, and to these one must bow.

In order to seize hold of the fantasies, I frequently imagined a steep descent ... a *crater ... I had the feeling that I was in the land of the dead.... I caught sight of two figures, an old man with a white beard and a beautiful young girl.... She was blind.... What a strange couple: Salome and Elijah. But Elijah assured me that he and Salome had belonged together from all eternity.... They had a black serpent living with them which displayed an unmistakable fondness for me.*

In myths the snake is a frequent counterpart of the hero.... Elijah is the wise old prophet ... the factor of intelligence and knowledge; Salome, the erotic element ... an anima figure ... blind because she does not see the meaning of things.[66]

To hold any kind of balance between inner and outer self was a struggle.

I needed a point of support in "this world." ... The unconscious contents could have driven me out of my wits. But my family and the knowledge: I have a medical diploma from a Swiss university, I must help my patients, I have a wife and five children, I live at 228 Seestrasse in Küsnacht – these were actualities which made demands upon me....

My family and my profession always remained a joyful reality and a guarantee that I also had a normal existence.[67]

Toni Wolff, December 1930.

Patient, student, poet, muse, love, friend, and colleague, Toni worked with Jung for most of her life.

TONI

A "point of support" not mentioned in *Memories, Dreams, Reflections*, as published, was Toni Wolff, a former patient, lyric poet, and later therapist whom Jung described to Freud in 1911 as

> a new discovery ... a remarkable intellect with an excellent feeling for religion and philosophy.[68]

Thirteen years younger than Jung, it was she who initiated a personal relationship with him, introduced him to Eastern spirituality, helped free his intuition from the bonds of his intellect, and brought him back to everyday reality if he was losing himself. It could be said that Toni Wolff was the reflection of Jung's feminine and undiscovered self, the bridge and guiding force of his period of crisis.

> Either she did not love me and was indifferent concerning my fate, or she loved me – as she certainly did – and then it was nothing short of heroism. Such things stand forever, and I shall be grateful to her in all eternity.[69]

Emma Jung is reported to have said near the end of her life,

> I shall always be grateful to Toni for doing for my husband what I or anyone could not have done for him at a most critical time.[70]

Their relationship, personal and professional, was to run parallel to Jung's marriage for forty years. It was lived openly, though often with painful difficulties in the early stages for both women, until an acceptable way of living was found. It was in later years that Emma confided to a friend,

> You see, he never took anything from me to give to Toni, but the more he gave her the more he seemed able to give me.[71]

BREAKTHROUGH

But in Jung's midlife struggle for himself there was not much to give out to his family. It was he himself who still needed all the support he could find. Insomnia and stomach trouble accompanied the intense suffering of this period. The fear of losing his hold remained as new fantasy figures rose out of his unconscious mind in dreams. Only now they didn't seem to personify aspects of his personal life.

a blue sky, like the sea, covered ... by flat brown clods of earth
... breaking apart ... suddenly ... a winged being sailing across
the sky ... an old man with the horns of a bull. He held a bunch
of four keys, one ... clutched as if he were about to open a lock.
He had the wings of a kingfisher with its characteristic colors.

Philemon was a pagan and brought with him an Egypto-Hellenic atmosphere with a Gnostic coloration.[72]

While painting this dream image Jung was "thunderstruck" to find, in his garden, a newly dead kingfisher with no signs of external injuries, a rare experience in Zürich. It was the kind of meaningful coincidence he was to call "synchronicity."

Philemon and other figures of my fantasies brought home to me the crucial insight that there are things in the psyche which I do

Neo-Babylonian seal of a winged hero, c. 800 BCE.
Jung's vision-figure Philemon was a winged spirit based on the ancient archetype of the wise counselor.

ABOVE *The Deceased Standing Before a Ka on a Pedestal*; from the *Papyrus of Nu*, Egypt. The hieroglyphic sign of *ka* ⊔̣ (LEFT *ka* from a plate of rolled papyrus) was the ancient Egyptian designation for the generating and sustaining vital forces, especially of men, and was later extended to denote the spiritual life-force in general. The *ka*-gesture, made by raising the open hands with palms facing outward, served as protection, and the hieroglyph for *ka* had the same effect.

not produce, but which produce themselves and have their own life. Philemon represented a force which was not myself…. It was he who taught me psychic objectivity, the reality of the psyche…. I understood that there is something in me which can say things that I do not know and do not intend….

Psychologically, Philemon represented superior insight…. To me he was what the Indians call a guru….

And the fact was that he conveyed to me many an illuminating idea.[73]

A final fantasy was a figure from deep out of the earth whom Jung called Ka. In ancient Egypt it was the name given to the king's earthly form, his "embodied soul."

I did a painting of him, showing him in his earth-bound form, as a herm with base of stone and upper part of bronze…. Ka's expression has something demonic about it…. He is saying, "I am he who buries the gods in gold and gems."

Philemon had a lame foot, but was a winged spirit, whereas Ka represented a kind of earth demon…. Philemon was the spiritual aspect, or "meaning." Ka … was a spirit of nature….

Ka was he who made everything real, but who also obscured the halcyon spirit, Meaning, or replaced it by beauty....

In time I was able to integrate both figures through the study of alchemy.[74]

From the safe distance in time of his autobiography, Jung could conclude

It is of course ironical that I, a psychiatrist, should at almost every step of my experiment have run into the same psychic material which is the stuff of psychosis and is found in the insane. This is the fund of unconscious images which fatally confuse the mental patient. But it is also the matrix of a mythopoeic imagination which has vanished from our rational age. Though such imagination is present everywhere, it is both tabooed and dreaded.[75]

In 1916, while a rational age reaped half a million deaths in war, a very gradual inner change began for Jung. This prelude to emergence urged creative form to what might have been taught by Philemon. The lead-up to the book *Seven Sermons to the Dead* involved the whole Jung household in what seemed to be a haunting by ghostly entities.

Around five o'clock in the afternoon on Sunday the front doorbell began ringing frantically. It was a bright summer day; the two maids were in the kitchen, from which the open square outside the front door could be seen. Everyone immediately looked to see who was there, but there was no one in sight. I was sitting near the doorbell, and not only heard it but saw it moving. We all simply stared at one another. The atmosphere was thick, believe me! Then I knew that something had to happen. The whole house was filled as if there were a crowd present, crammed full of spirits. They were packed deep right up to the door, and the air was so thick it was scarcely possible to breathe. As for myself, I was all a-quiver with the question: "For God's sake, what in the world is this?" Then they cried out in chorus, "We have come back from Jerusalem where we found not what we sought." That is the beginning of the Seven Sermons.

Then it began to flow out of me, and in the course of three evenings the thing was written. As soon as I took up the pen, the whole ghostly assemblage evaporated.... The haunting was over....

These conversations with the dead formed a kind of prelude to what I had to communicate to the world about the unconscious: a kind of pattern of order and interpretation of its general contents.[76]

The book is a kind of poem written in archaic style. *Seven Sermons to the Dead* was originally published anonymously in limited edition and is not included, by his own request, in the official twenty volumes of *Jung's Collected Works*. Yet it outlines the skeleton of his most essential ideas, including the conflict of opposites and the concept of individuation.

There is a god whom ye know not, for mankind forgot it. We name it by its name Abraxas. It is more indefinite still than god and devil.... It is improbable probability, unreal reality. Had the pleroma a being, Abraxas would be its manifestation....

It is also creatura, because it is distinct from the pleroma....

The power of Abraxas is twofold; but ye see it not, because for your eyes the warring opposites of this power are extinguished.

What the god-sun speaketh is life.

What the devil speaketh is death.

But Abraxas speaketh that hallowed and accursed word which is life and death at the same time.

Abraxas begetteth truth and lying, good and evil, light and darkness, in the same word and in the same act. Wherefore is Abraxas terrible....

It is abundance that seeketh union with emptiness.

It is holy begetting.

It is love and love's murder.

It is the saint and his betrayer.

It is the brightest light of day and darkest

Abraxas; design from a Gnostic gem, second century. Jung wore a Gnostic signet ring. Abraxas is the Gnostic deity whose name, in the Greek Kabbala, equates to 365 – the number of days in the year. Hence he is a solar deity. His rooster's head confirms this attribution. Abraxas combines good and evil in a unity. The serpents that form his legs imply a creative, sexual aspect.

night of madness....

It is the mightiest creature, and in it the creature is afraid of itself.

It is the manifest opposition of creatura to the pleroma and its nothingness....

It is the life of creatura.

It is the operation of distinctiveness.

It is the love of man....

It is the appearance and the shadow of man.

It is illusory reality.[77]

If Jung's sense of isolation began with the experience of childhood dreams it peaked in the years of inner images. He had been compelled to go through an unconscious process, not knowing what it meant or where it led. The gulf between inner and outer worlds seemed irreconcilable, their interaction not yet seen.

Dim understanding began in the last two years of the war while he was stationed as Medical Corps Doctor and Commander of a British internment camp in Switzerland. Every morning he sketched in a notebook a circular drawing which seemed to correspond to his inner situation at the time. He called them *mandalas*, the Sanskrit word for circle. Mandalas show a diversity of patterns radiating from a central point. Jung discovered them to be universal symbols of the energy of the human form.

With the help of these drawings I could observe my psychic transformations from day to day.... My mandalas were cryptograms concerning the state of the self.... In them I saw the self – that is, my whole being – actively at work. To be sure, at first I could only dimly understand them, but they seemed to me highly significant, and I guarded them like precious pearls. I had the distinct feeling that they were something central....

Only gradually did I discover what the mandala really is: "Formation, Transformation, Eternal Mind's eternal recreation" and that is the self, the wholeness of the personality....

The self, I thought, was like the monad which I am, and which is my world. The mandala represents this monad, and corresponds to the microcosmic nature of the psyche.[78]

Jung's entire inner journey is recorded by him in *The Red Book*, written in calligraphic script and illustrated with numerous paintings of what he experienced.

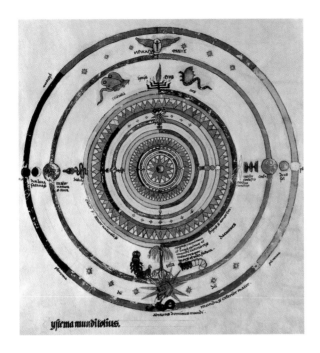

Systema Munditotius; painting by C.G. Jung, 1916.

Jung's first mandala, from *The Red Book*, pictures the self complete and in relationship to the universe.

The Red Book, including Seven Sermons to the Dead, was published in 2009 as a facsimile of the original.

The years when I was pursuing my inner images were the most important in my life – in them everything essential was decided....

It was then that I ceased to belong to myself alone, ceased to have the right to do so. From then on, my life belonged to the generality. The knowledge I was concerned with, or was seeking, still could not be found in the science of those days. I myself had to undergo the original experience, and, moreover, try to plant the results of my experience in the soil of reality.... It was then that I dedicated myself to service of the psyche. I loved and hated it, but it was my greatest wealth. My delivering of myself over to it ... was the only way by which I could endure my existence and live it as fully as possible....

It has taken me virtually forty-five years to distill within the vessel of my scientific work the things I experienced and wrote down at that time.... That was the primal stuff which compelled me to work upon it.... It was the *prima materia* for a lifetime's work.[79]

PART TWO

HEALER

I have an old soul. At high school at fifteen, my schoolmates called me the Patriarch Abraham. That's very important, an old soul. We always retain traces of an existence which is not earthly, a state of abundance where we know everything.[1]

PAGE 80: *Bow to Creativity*; painting by C.G. Jung, from *The Red Book*.
ABOVE: Jung in his eighties.

PRELUDE

Carl Jung has been called the first New Age psychologist. His entire work has been described as "a psycho-religious statement, a progressive interpretation of the numinous by which man is consciously or unconsciously filled, surrounded and led."[2]

Jung fought off all attempts to label him a "mystic." Repeatedly he defined himself as "an empiricist who moved within the limits of a natural empirical science."

Central to his Analytical Psychology is the individuation process. It might also be called "coming to selfhood" or "self-realization."

The individual is all-important as he is the carrier of life, and his development and fulfillment are of paramount significance. It is vital for each living being to become its own entelechia and to grow into that which it was from the very beginning.[3]

Individuation is the experience of a natural law, an inner self-regulating process by which man becomes a whole human being acknowledging and living the total

Detail from *Creation of Adam*; fresco by Michelangelo Buonarroti, Sistine Chapel, Vatican, Rome, c. 1511–1512.
Individuation means that a man becomes an adult, knowing "that he does not only depend on God but that God also depends on man."

The Dream; detail of painting by Frantisek Kupka, *c.* 1909.
To individuals, becoming whole or complete is the process by which we "give birth" to
ourselves as both "truly human" and "partially divine" within the Self.

range of himself. In the process the ego is ultimately faced with something larger
than itself, a force that it yields to and serves. The human being thus recognizes itself
as both material and spiritual, conscious and unconscious.

Individuation does not only mean that man has become truly
human as distinct from animal, but that he is to become partially
divine as well. That means practically that he becomes adult,

responsible for his existence, knowing that he does not only depend on God but that God also depends on man.[4]

Jung was at some pains to point out that the wholeness he spoke of meant completion, not perfection. Perfection he saw as a masculine concept, completion as a feminine one.

To get integrated or complete is such a formidable task that one does not dare to set people further goals like perfection. As for instance the ordinary physician neither imagines nor hopes to make of his patient an ideal athlete, so the psychological doctor does not dream of being able to produce saints. He is highly content if he brings forth in himself as well as in others a fairly balanced and more or less sound individual, no matter how far from the state of perfection. Before we strive after perfection, we ought to be able to live the ordinary man without self-mutilation. If anybody should find himself after his humble completion still left with a sufficient amount of energy, then he may begin his career as a saint.[5]

In 1921 Jung's book *Psychological Types* was published, introducing the term "introverted" and "extroverted" into everyday speech as basic categories of typology with four psychological functions – thinking, feeling, sensation, and intuition. At about the same time he was a speaker in the "School of Wisdom" lectures put on by his friend Count Herman Keyserling in Germany. Participants were an eclectic mix of representatives from diverse fields including psychiatry, philosophy, and anthropology.

Social worker Olga Freun von König-Fachsenfeld was one of them.

In an atmosphere that was, I might say, almost prickly with intellect and also a bit modish, the lectures kept offering new high points. But it was the statements of C.G. Jung, then still unknown to me, that touched me in a quite special way. They contrasted so thoroughly with the rational intellectuality of the rest – at least that was my impression. But, simultaneously with my admiring fascination, my young sense of reality became alerted. "This is 'superbrain', can this be all right?"

When later in the course of the session I saw Jung, like a sturdy peasant, his hat pushed back to the scruff of his neck,

Photograph by Toni Wolff.
Jung in "peasant" cap at a seminar in Swanage, England, 1925.

walking out of that convivial [fashionable] society milieu in long
strides, then I knew: "If this man says something like that, then
it must be all right." The earth-rootedness that I felt in Jung was
for me the guarantee for the credibility of his psychology.[6]

PRIMAL CULTURES

Jung was already making a series of expeditions into territories where no European language was spoken, no Christian concepts prevailed, and rational intellect was not a guiding ideal. He needed to see European culture from the outside. A couple of visits to Africa produced vitalizing impressions that he drew on for decades.

Dr. Henry Fierz remembered this story from his father, who was with Jung in Alexandria.

> When they left the boat a chiromancer came to them and offered to read their hands.... He read Jung's....
>
> "Oh, you are one of the very few great men I have seen. I can't say more." And he added "For great men and their friends there is no fee," but he got something of course.[7]

Jung has left some vivid accounts of the effects of his travels on him.

> From Tozeur I went on to the oasis of Nefta.... Our mounts were large, swift-footed mules, on which we made rapid progress. As we approached the oasis, a single rider, wholly swathed in

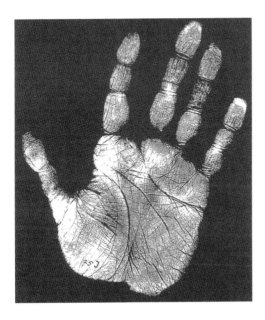

Jung's handprint.
This print shows both extraordinary physical strength and deep wellsprings of imaginative thought.

Portrait of Vollard; painting by Pablo Picasso, 1910.

Jung contrasted the vitality and self-possession of Africans and Native Americans he encountered in his travels with fragmented Europeans, out of contact with their center.

white, came toward us. With proud bearing he rode by without offering us any greeting, mounted on a black mule whose harness was banded and studded with silver. He made an impressive, elegant figure. Here was a man who certainly possessed no pocket watch, let alone a wrist watch; for he was obviously and unselfconsciously the person he had always been. He lacked that faint note of foolishness which clings to the European. The European is, to be sure, convinced that he is no longer what he was ages ago; but he does not know what he has since become. His watch tells him that since the "Middle Ages" time and its synonym, progress, have crept up on him and irrevocably taken something from him. With lightened baggage he continues his journey, with steadily increasing velocity, toward nebulous goals. He compensates for the loss of gravity and the corresponding *sentiment d'incomplétude* by the illusion of his triumphs, such as steamships, railways, aeroplanes, and rockets, that rob him of his duration and transport him into another reality of speeds and explosive accelerations.

The deeper we penetrated into the Sahara, the more time slowed down for me; it even threatened to move backward.[8]

From this he could see that Europeans had gained "a certain measure of will and directed intention" at the cost of "intensity of life." The rationalist too found "much that is human alien to him." The result was a loss of vitality and a forcing underground of primitive parts of the psyche. This kind of cut-off European he would describe as a "technological savage" and "intellectual barbarian." Around him

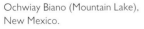

Ochwiay Biano (Mountain Lake), New Mexico.

A Pueblo Chief befriended Jung in 1924 and brought home to him the truth of thinking with the heart.

Eagle Dancer, painting by Pablita Velarde, Santa Clara Pueblo, twentieth century.
The Pueblo Indian, through the connection he maintains with his winged brothers and its attendant ritual, helps keep the earth in balance.

in North Africa people lived "so much closer to life," their lives and being centered in emotion.

On a trip to Taos, New Mexico, a Pueblo Indian Chief, Ochwiay Biano (Mountain Lake), brought the point home very directly to Jung.

"See," Ochwiay Biano said, "how cruel the whites look. Their lips are thin, their noses sharp, their faces furrowed and distorted by folds. Their eyes have a staring expression; they are always seeking something. What are they seeking? The whites always want something; they are always uneasy and restless. We do not know what they want. We do not understand them. We think that they are mad."

I asked him why he thought the whites were all mad.

"They say that they think with their heads," he replied. "Why of course. What do you think with?" I asked him in surprise.

"We think here," he said, indicating his heart.

I fell into a long meditation. For the first time in my life, so it seemed to me, someone had drawn for me a picture of the real white man.... This Indian had struck our vulnerable spot, unveiled a truth to which we are blind....

What we from our point of view call colonization, missions to the heathen, spread of civilization, etc., has another face – the face of a bird of prey seeking with cruel intentness for distant quarry – a face worthy of a race of pirates and highwaymen....

After a prolonged silence he continued, "The Americans want to stamp out our religion. Why can they not let us alone? What we do, we do not only for ourselves but for the Americans also. Yes, we do it for the whole world. Everyone benefits by it."

I could observe from his excitement that he was alluding to some extremely important element of his religion. I therefore asked him: "You think, then, that what you do in your religion benefits the whole world?" He replied with great animation, "Of course. If we did not do it, what would become of the world?" And with a significant gesture he pointed to the sun....

"After all," he said, "we are a people who live on the roof of the world; we are the sons of Father Sun, and with our religion we daily help our father to go across the sky." ...

I then realized on what the "dignity," the tranquil composure of the individual Indian, was founded ... his life is cosmologically meaningful, for he helps the father and preserver of all life in his daily rise and descent.... Out of sheer envy we are obliged to smile at the Indians' naïveté and to plume ourselves on our cleverness; for otherwise we would discover how impoverished and down at the heels we are. Knowledge does not enrich us; it removes us more and more from the mythic world in which we were once at home by right of birth.[9]

Equatorial Africa captured Jung for life. What he called the "divine peace" of a still-primeval country stirred those elements in himself, the "immemorially known," bringing into focus a major realization on the Athi Plains, a game preserve near Nairobi.

To the very brink of the horizon we saw gigantic herds of animals: gazelle, antelope, gnu, zebra, warthog, and so on. Grazing, heads nodding, the herds moved forward like slow rivers. There was scarcely any sound save the melancholy cry of a bird of prey. This was the stillness of the eternal beginning, the world as it had always been, in the state of non-being; for until then no one had been present to know that it was this world....

There the cosmic meaning of consciousness became overwhelmingly clear to me.... Man, I, in an invisible act of creation put the stamp of perfection on the world by giving it objective existence. This act we usually ascribe to the Creator alone, without considering that in so doing we view life as a machine calculated down to the last detail, which, along with the human psyche, runs on senselessly, obeying foreknown and predetermined rules. In such a cheerless clockwork fantasy there is no drama of man, world, and God; there is no "new day" leading to "new shores," but only the dreariness of calculated processes. My old Pueblo friend came to my mind. He thought that the raison d'être of his pueblo had been to help their father, the sun, to cross the sky each day. I had envied him for the fullness of meaning in that belief, and had been looking about without hope for a myth of our own. Now I knew what it was, and knew even more: that man is indispensable for the completion of creation; that, in fact, he himself is the second creator of the world....[10]

Map of What Is Effortless; gouache by Francesco Clemente, 1978.
On the Athi Plains, a great game preserve in Africa, Jung came to recognize a cosmic meaning for modern man: The human being, as witness and participant, "is indispensable for the completion of creation."

ABOVE: Tower at Bollingen, which Jung helped build, after the second phase of construction.

"At Bollingen," he said, "I am most deeply myself."

LEFT: Jung at Bollingen.

Of lighting lanterns, water-pumping, wood-cutting, firemaking, and cooking, Jung said, "These simple acts make man simple."

BOLLINGEN

Back in Switzerland, Jung set about creating a retreat for himself, a second home expressing in concrete form his inner nature. Bollingen, at lake's edge in Zürich, twenty miles and light years from his family home in Küsnacht, is a medieval monument of towers and turrets, stone and silence, inviting the solitude he needed. He built the first tower after his mother's death in 1923, adding new sections over a thirty-two-year period. Over the original door is chiselled in stone, "Sanctuary of Philemon, penitence of Faust."

The feeling of repose and renewal that I had in this tower was intense from the start. It represented for me the maternal hearth ... in which I could become what I was, what I am and will be.... At Bollingen I am in the midst of my true life, I am most deeply myself. Here I am, as it were, the "age-old son of the mother" ... personality No. 2, who ... exists outside time....

I have done without electricity, and tend the fireplace and stove myself. Evenings, I light the old lamps. There is no running water, and I pump the water from the well. I chop the wood and cook the food. These simple acts make man simple; and how difficult it is to be simple!

In Bollingen, silence surrounds me almost audibly, and I live "in modest harmony with nature." Thoughts rise to the surface which reach back into the centuries, and accordingly anticipate a remote future....

There I ... see life in the round, as something forever coming into being and passing on.[11]

METAPHORS

Jung's thinking deepened. Mythology, archetypes, and the collective unconscious clarified as concepts and linked together. Myths are metaphors, "descriptions of psychic processes and development" which "connect us with the instinctive bases of our existence." Mythic ideas can be observed worldwide in mythology, fairy tales, and "in the dreams, visions and fantasies of normal and psychically ill persons."

While the intellect may see mythologizing as "futile speculation," to the emotions it is "a healing and valid activity" which "expresses life more precisely than science" and allows it to be lived out more innately than through a manmade code of ethics.

An ethical fraternity, with its mythical Nothing, not infused by

any archaic-infantile driving force, is a pure vacuum and can never evoke in man the slightest trace of that age-old animal power which drives the migrating bird across the sea....[12]

Moreover, he wrote, mythic life demands "a going beyond." Its symbolic language gives "unimaginable" religious experience "an image, a form in which to express itself."

Myth is the revelation of a divine life in man. It is not we who invent myth, rather it speaks to us as a Word of God.[13]

Myths arise from the archetypes, "primordial ideas of humanity," "basic patterns of instinct" which occur universally, "an imprint which implies an imprinter."

The archetypes ... are not intellectually invented. They are always there and they produce certain processes in the unconscious one could best compare with myths. That's the origin of mythology. Mythology is a dramatization of a series of images that formulate the life of the archetypes.[14]

The archetypal "pattern" is to the unconscious what the biological pattern is to the body. The archetypes together form the structure of the collective unconscious, the counterpart in the psyche to the collective conscious mind.

Preparing the Elixir of Life; woodcut of alchemical laboratory, Strasbourg, 1528.
Jung studied the symbolic language of alchemy, a European tradition of transformative processes that unites opposites to bring forth living knowledge.

HISTORICAL
COUNTERPARTS

Jung developed his ideas very much in isolation from the professional milieu of the day. Yet slowly he began to find parallels to his thinking elsewhere. Discarded Gnostic texts from early Christian times occupied him for eight years. The Gnostics too "had been confronted with the primal world of the unconscious and had dealt with its contents." But there were big gaps in the texts, and the time lapse of nearly 1,800 years between their writing and the twentieth century was too wide to bridge.

Then, in 1928, Oriental scholar Richard Wilhelm sent Jung a medieval manuscript of Chinese yoga and alchemy, *The Secret of the Golden Flower*, requesting him to write a psychological commentary on it. To Jung it brought "undreamed-of confirmation" of his own ideas.

I had stumbled upon the historical counterpart of my psychology of the unconscious. The possibility of a comparison with alchemy, and the uninterrupted intellectual chain back to Gnosticism, gave substance to my psychology. When I pored over these old texts everything fell into place: the fantasy-images, the empirical material I had gathered in my practice, and the conclusions I had drawn from it.... My understanding of their typical character, which had already begun with my investigation of myths, was deepened. The primordial images and the nature of the archetype took a central place in my researches....[15]

Alchemy had already announced itself to Jung years earlier in a dream which he had not at that time understood. Learning to decipher the symbolic language of alchemy from sixteenth- and seventeenth-century manuscripts absorbed him for more than a decade. Alchemy too faced the problem of matter, the feminine principle, and the union of opposites: masculine and feminine, God and human being.

Only after I had familiarized myself with alchemy did I realize that the unconscious is a *process*, and that the psyche is transformed or developed by the relationship of the ego to the contents of the unconscious. In individual cases that transformation can be read from dreams and fantasies. In collective life it has left its deposit

Consecration by Horus and Set of Seti I; tracing of papyrus, Thebes, Nineteenth Dynasty, *c.* 1250 BCE. The deities are showering the pharaoh, Seti I, with Ankhs poured forth from the vases held in their hands. The Ankh is a symbol of life, fertility, and immortality. The Water of Life is poured over the initiate to symbolize his rebirth into new universal knowledge.

principally in the various religious systems and their changing symbols. Through the study of these collective transformation processes and through understanding of alchemical symbolism I arrived at the central concept of my psychology: *the process of individuation*.[16]

For Jung, reaching to the "spiritual East" was not a replacement of Western culture but rather a filling of gaps in both it and ourselves, "a symbolic expression of the fact that we are entering into connection with the elements in ourselves which are strange to us."

In a letter he explained,

You rightly say that it is as if my work "reached out beyond philosophy and theology." You could also say it begins "behind" both of them. But it is not due to any intention or activity of mine that the spiritual and historical analogy with the East gets into my way of looking at things.... It is not, however, the actual East we are dealing with but the collective unconscious, which is omnipresent.... I have landed in the Eastern sphere through the waters of the unconscious, for the truths of the unconscious can never be thought up, they can be reached only by following a path which all cultures right down to the most primitive level have called the way of initiation.[17]

REMINISCENCES

Analyst and author Jane Wheelwright was a patient of Jung's in the 1930s.

Jung was a mountain of a man – big enough to encompass every kind of person imaginable. All kinds of people big and small found through him their uniqueness. He touched all kinds of people who came his way. Sometimes it was through what he inadvertently said – more often than not something he would not remember. Sometimes it was what he did. Mostly it was what he was: a comprehensive, large, all-embracing, complete man. He spanned in himself everything from greatness and power to all-too-human failings. He could be irritable and sometimes downright demanding. Explosions of rage were not uncommon. He even could be duped at times by unscrupulous, ambitious people. Sometimes he seemed to reduce to human ordinariness. At other times he seemed to expand – to literally physically expand – to overpowering size. I remember once experiencing him like this. I must have betrayed my feeling that he was beyond my reach because he said out of the blue, "Do I have horns on my head?" Jung was able to constellate the unconscious of countless numbers and kinds of people. It was an extraordinary gift that he had.... I believe he was at his best as an analyst.[18]

In Barbara Hannah's biographical memoir of Jung she said,

One of Jung's most striking characteristics was the fact that he never asked anything of people that he had not first asked of himself, and he told me once, when he was nearly sixty,

Jung at Bailey Island, Maine, 1936.
"Jung was a mountain of a man – big enough to encompass every kind of person imaginable."

that he could say his whole life had been spent in eliminating his own childishness. He added ruefully, with that uncompromising honesty that was so convincing, that he was afraid there was still quite a bit left.[19]

Jung has publicly acknowledged his own debt to his patients – most of them women.

From my encounters with patients and with the psychic phenomena which they have paraded before me in an endless stream of images, I have learned an enormous amount – not just knowledge, but above all insight into my own nature. And not the least of what I have learned has come from my errors and defeats. I have had mainly women patients, who often entered into the work with extraordinary conscientiousness, understanding, and intelligence. It was essentially because of them that I was able to strike out on new paths in therapy.[20]

Former patient Elizabeth Shepley Sergeant has left this account of a consultation:

Doctor Jung's patients must take a little steamboat at a landing haunted by gulls and wild ducks, and then walk a good ten minutes to a yellow country house standing well within walls and gardens.... They must pull a shining brass bell and ... meet the inspection of a group of skirmishing dogs.

Yoggi, the Doctor's special intimate, always manages to slide into the upstairs study behind the visitor.... I noticed at my first interview that Jung's hand – the sensitive,

Jung on the porch of a library on Bailey Island, Maine, 1936.
Bailey Island was a resort where Jung held a summer seminar. A patient of his in the 1930s felt his energy akin to Theodore Roosevelt, and his appearance to be "more like a stockbroker than a prophet."

Krishna Battling the Horse Demon, Keshi; terracotta, India, fifth century.
The god and animal selves in combat. At nearly sixty, Jung admitted to a lifelong battle with his own demon of "childishness," which was still a continuing threat.

strong hand, with the Gnostic ring – reached down now and then to the shaggy back. And it came to me that this touch with an instinctive hairy being was somehow the riposte to the psychologist's uncanny intuition, his probing mind, his acute awareness a reassurance to the visitor and to himself. For what is one to think of a doctor who, in a hunch of the shoulders, a half-glance, a witty phrase casually spoken – "You are like an egg without a shell" – can say enough to keep one guessing for a week?

It was comfortable too, that as he discussed intimate problems, his face now very sober and concerned, Jung tramped the floor, fed the fire, lighted a meditative pipe: common clay and spirit were all one. When he sat stiffly in his chair for a moment and gulped down his tea, he suddenly turned into a German professor. But when his eyes began to twinkle merrily behind their gold-rimmed spectacles, when he moved about again, his driving energy strongly held in leash, I thought of Theodore Roosevelt. "You look more like a stockbroker than a prophet," exclaimed a startled American who had expected to find the "mystic" of Freudian report. The actual Jung, solid and vital in his middle fifties, humorous and skeptical, refuses to stand on a pedestal or to take on any white-bearded Old Testament air. "Yes," he agrees with a young lady, "all men are liars, certainly. I just let them sit in that chair and lie till they get tired of lying. Then they begin to tell the truth." One leaves Jung's presence feeling enriched and appeased, as by contact with a pine tree in the forest, a life as much below ground as above.[21]

And from Jane Wheelwright again:

I had come to Zürich, stuck in a kind of modern hopelessness and isolation and two-dimensional ordinariness that seemed inevitable. Then, suddenly in Zürich, at last, there was life – even though at times it was expressed in strange, sometimes weird ways.[22]

THE INDIVIDUATION PROCESS

"People," Jung observed, "live on only one or two floors of a large apartment building which is our minds, forgetting the rest." The individuation process puts us in touch with "the rest." Our conscious "I" is not the total psyche. There is an unconscious background that operates subliminally, whether we realize it or not. Plugging into those undertones and making them conscious enlarges and deepens our experience of ourselves and of life. The unconscious can be guide, friend, and adviser to the conscious. It speaks to us in the language of symbols, usually in the form of dreams.

Going inward means looking for the signs and symbols the unconscious dreams up for us naturally and spontaneously. Analyzing, interpreting, and synthesizing them into our being is the work of our conscious selves. The world of the unconscious is essentially an ambivalent one, with both negative and positive aspects at all its

The Six Elements; oil painting by René Magritte, 1929.
Jung said that we live in only one or two sections of our conscious selves and are out of touch with everything else within us. The individuation process prods us into awareness of our unconscious nature as it speaks to us in the language of symbols, observed mainly in our dreams.

Blue Shadow Spirit; detail of painting by Frank LaPena, Wintu/ Nomtipom, 1991. For each of us the shadow is a call to explore our lives in greater depth. Bringing it into light and dealing with its contents, whatever they may be, helps us to grow into a larger sense of our humanity.

levels, which doesn't make it easy to understand. Often it begins to make itself felt out of a negative state, such as boredom or stagnation in life, or a blow to the ego, a wounding of the personality.

The first layer we encounter in the unconscious is what Jung called the shadow, usually those parts of ourselves we don't like, don't know, or don't want to know. The shadow can be repressed in us like a cancer or projected outward onto others as qualities we dislike most in a person or group. The negative shadow can present us with a shortcoming to be overcome. The positive can show us a meaningful part of ourselves we should recognize and live out. Either way it's a tricky element to deal with, as Jung himself knew.

You may shake your head incredulously when I tell you that I would hardly have been able to form the concept of the shadow had not its existence become one of my greatest experiences, not just with regard to other people but with regard to myself....

My shadow is indeed so huge that I could not possibly

overlook it in the plan of my life; in fact I had to see it as an essential part of my personality, accept the consequences of this realization, and take responsibility for them. Many bitter circumstances have forced me to see that though the sin one has committed or is can be regretted, it is not canceled out. I don't believe in the tiger who was finally converted to vegetarianism and ate only apples. My solace was always Paul, who did not deem it beneath his dignity to admit he bore a thorn in the flesh.[23]

Psychotherapist Elizabeth Howes retained this personal impression from talks with Jung:

This man did in fact accept the shadow and ... this acceptance brought problems and tensions but also aliveness, reality, integrity, and depth of being.[24]

But as Jung explained in a letter,

Recognizing the shadow is what I call the apprenticeship. But making out with the anima is what I call the masterpiece which not many bring off.[25]

It is only through knowledge of the shadow that we reach this next layer of the psyche: *anima*, the female image within a man, or *animus*, the male part of a woman.

Bronze sculpture (aquamanile), Netherlands, c. 1400. For a man, acceptance of his anima brings a balance between outer and inner self; for a woman, her complementary animus gives a strong foundational base for living.

Column capital,
Bamberg Cathedral,
Bamberg, Germany.
Photo by Clive Hicks.
The Green Man, a
European vegetative
spirit, is an archetypal
animus figure, potent
and generative. Although
pre-Christian, he
found his way into the
Church by appearing in
hidden places of sacred
buildings.

Anima is the soul image of a man represented in dreams or fantasies by a feminine figure. It symbolizes the function of relationship. The animus is the image of spiritual forces in a woman, symbolized by a masculine figure. If a man or woman is unconscious of these inner forces, they appear in a projection.[26]

The anima is influenced by the experience of the mother, the animus by the father, with effects that can be negative or positive. Images of the anima can range from primitive woman to romanticized beauty, the Virgin Mary as spiritualized Eros, or a goddess of wisdom as mediator to the world within. The animus can be personified, or projected, as physical Tarzan, romantic poet, man of action, political power hero, or wise guide to spiritual truth and meaning.

Writer Margaret Flinters went to Jung when he was still formulating the anima/animus terms of his psychology. She was then a person alienated from husband, family, work, and the world.

Bringing me down to earth ... was literally the problem and he succeeded brilliantly. I don't know how he did it quite. First of all

I think it was his own peasant solidity which gave me the feeling I was in touch with a real man for the first time in my life. All the others were wraiths. Second – I suppose – he made me see that I had a ghost somewhere inside me, directing me. It was what he later called the animus, a sort of archetypal animus-figure of the father of all nature. My own father – who was a perfectionist – wouldn't have any truck with anything which didn't match up to the best standards. That was part of my trouble too. My husband fell short of my ideal. My writing was not perfect. I was afraid of having a child in case it wasn't brilliant. I don't clearly understand transference – but something like that took place – Jung becoming a much more tolerant, much less exacting father figure – and of course the repressed love I had for my father burst out all over him and he found it – I know – damned inconvenient. It must have been a terrible trial to him.[27]

In *Civilization in Transition*, Jung wrote,

A human relationship leads into the world of the psyche, into that intermediate realm between sense and spirit, which contains something of both and yet forfeits nothing of its own unique character.

Into this territory a man must venture if he wishes to meet woman half way. Circumstances have forced her to acquire a number of masculine traits, so that she shall not remain caught in an

Couple; wood carving, Dogon people, Mali. To grow together and bring about completion in relationship, both man and woman can help develop in the one the gifts of the other.

antiquated, purely instinctual femininity, lost and alone in the world of men. So, too, man will be forced to develop his feminine side, to open his eyes to the psyche and to Eros. It is a task he cannot avoid....[28]

The path inward is largely via dreams, which Jung described as "the invisible roots of our conscious thoughts."

He told Laurens van der Post that he worked through 67,000 dreams with patients and helpers before even attempting to theorize about them. "Dreams," he said "are facts," "specific expressions of our unconscious" which "somehow make sense." In them the unconscious is trying to become conscious. It uses symbols common to all mankind in an entirely individual way. The dreamer holds the personal "key" to interpretation. The ability to establish communication with the unconscious is part of the whole person.

Dreams reflect many layers of our psyche. At surface level they can show personal contents that have been absorbed subliminally or pushed from the conscious to the upper end of the unconscious. They can also tell us more about ourselves, about other people or events. They can project forward as well as backward in time. From deeper in, new contents can arise revealing creative ideas or germs of future emotional conditions in our psyche.

Then there are the "big" archetypal dreams of the collective unconscious, often using symbols of a religious or mythological nature and numinously tinged. The meandering pattern of dreams, observed over a long period of time, reveals the gradual degrees of psychic growth that characterize the individuation process. This inner growth then slowly emerges into conscious life as a fuller and more mature personality.

Active imagination was the method invented by Jung to amplify and activate dream or fantasy images. It is a way of meditating imaginatively, without conscious goal or program, on objective hints being thrown up by the unconscious.

The initial question to be directed ... would be: "Who or what has come alive? ... Who or what has entered my psychic life and created disturbances and wants to be heard?" To this you should add: "Let it speak!" Then switch off your noisy consciousness and listen quietly inward and look at the images that appear before your inner eye, or hearken to the words which the muscles of your speech apparatus are trying to form. Write down what then comes without criticism. Images should be drawn or painted assiduously no matter whether you can do it or not.

Memories; oil painting by Tobi Zausner, 1981.
Our dreams propel us into a landscape of universal symbols, which can speak both to our deepest personal realities and to the collective archetypal world that underpins them.

Once you have got at least fragments of these contents, then you may meditate on them afterwards. Don't criticize anything away! If any questions arise, put them to the unconscious again the next day. Don't be content with your own explanations no matter how intelligent they are....

Treat any drawings the same way. Meditate on them afterwards and every day go on developing what is unsatisfactory about them. The important thing is to let the unconscious take the lead.[29]

But the unconscious may not take over exclusively.

It is under all conditions a most advisable thing to keep to the conscious and rational side, i.e., to maintain that side. One never should lose sight of it. It is the safeguard without which you would lose yourself on unknown seas. You would invite illness, indeed, if you should give up your conscious and rational orientation. On the other hand, it is equally true that life is not

Toilers of the Sea; painting by Albert P. Ryder, c. 1915.
Jung has said that the unconscious, long identified as the oceanic in man, is Nature. The seeker of himself often feels cast adrift, setting a course between light and dark but ultimately moved along by unseen currents deep within.

only rational. To a certain extent you have to keep your senses open to the nonrational aspects of existence....

The unconscious itself is neither tricky nor evil – it is Nature, both beautiful and terrible.... The best way of dealing with the unconscious is the creative way....[30]

There is no point in delivering yourself over to the last drop.... In my view it is absolutely essential always to have our consciousness well enough in hand to pay sufficient attention to our reality, to the Here and Now.[31]

Active imagination, dreams, anima/animus, the shadow – they are all stations along the way to an acceptance of ourselves as we are, to letting life be. Jung quoted this letter from a former patient as a summing up of this "in simple and pertinent words."

> Out of evil, much good has come to me. By keeping quiet, repressing nothing, remaining attentive, and by accepting reality – taking things as they are, and not as I wanted them to be – by doing all this, unusual knowledge has come to me, and unusual powers as well, such as I could never have imagined before. I always thought that when we accepted things they overpowered us in some way or other. This turns out not to be true at all, and it is only by accepting them that one can assume an attitude toward them. So now I intend to play the game of life, being receptive to whatever comes to me, good and bad, sun

Wolf Devouring the King; alchemical engraving from *Atalanta Fugiens* by Michael Maier, Frankfurt, 1618.

Perhaps the process of life is to eat and be eaten – to experience the full range that exists between the ever-becoming and ever-dying in time. Freedom exists beyond the constant dichotomies.

and shadow that are forever alternating, and in this way, also accepting my own nature with its negative and positive sides. Thus everything becomes more alive to me. What a fool I was! How I tried to force everything to go according to the way I thought it ought to.[32]

Jung called this attitude "religious in the highest sense," adding that "only on the basis of such an attitude will a higher level of consciousness and culture be possible."[33]

By bearing the opposites we can expose ourselves to life in our humanity.... We have to realize the evil is in us; we have to risk life to get into life, then it takes on color, otherwise we might as well read a book....[34]

The opus consists of three parts; insight, endurance and action.... It is conflicts of duty that make endurance and action so difficult. The one must exist and so must the other. There can be no resolution, only patient endurance of the opposites, which ultimately spring from your own nature. You yourself are a conflict that rages in and against itself in order to melt its incompatible substances, the male and the female, in the fire of suffering and thus create that fixed and unalterable form which is the goal of life.... We are crucified between the opposites and delivered up to the torture until the reconciling third takes shape.[35]

The "reconciling third" that appears is the innermost nucleus of the psyche, the organizing center that includes the ego but is not defined by it, a transpersonal, transcendent reality

Enzo.
The Zen *enzo* embodies the all and the nothing. The emptiness enclosed is defined by the circle, but the circle itself is only the space that is "not a circle."

Nubian Tribute Bearer; ivory, Mesopotamia, eighth century BCE.
Jung reminds us that true psychic health demands true humanity, which is the ability to connect with and balance the inner and outer realities of life. We must accept both the god and the animal, seeking not to reject life's many aspects but to embrace them in full.

that Jung named the Self. The encounter with the Self is a centering which brings about a completion of the individuation process.

In a woman's dreams, the Self can be personified in female form as a priestess, earth mother, or goddess of love; in a man's it appears as a male guru, wise old man, or spirit of nature. This psychic image of the transcendent can also be Cosmic Man, a divine or royal couple, a person that is both male and female, young and old, or an animal, crystal, round stone, or mandala. Whatever the symbol, its meaning is wholeness, totality.

Jung quoted St. Bonaventure in defining his concept of the Self as "a circle whose center is everywhere and whose circumference is nowhere."

In a letter to Pastor Walter Bernet he enlarged further:

The goal seems to be anticipated by archetypal symbols which represent something like the circumambulation of a center. With increasing approximation to the center there is a corresponding depotentiation of the ego in favor of the influence of the "empty" center which is certainly not identical with the archetype but is the thing the archetype points to. As the Chinese would say, the archetype is only the name of Tao, not Tao itself. Just as the Jesuits translated Tao as "God," so we can describe the "emptiness" of the center as "god." Emptiness in this sense doesn't mean "absence" or "vacancy," but something unknowable which is endowed with the highest intensity.... I call this unknowable the Self.... The whole course of individuation is dialectical, and the so-called "end" is the confrontation of the ego with the "emptiness" of the center.[36]

"Everything essential," Jung said, "happens in the Self and the ego functions as a receiver, spectator, and transmitter."[37] "Free will is doing gladly and freely that which one must do."[38] It is the Self that gives the ego inner power for the creative renewal of life.

Nevertheless the Self, like all of life, has dual aspects, its worst being megalomania or a form of possession. Positive and negative have to be negotiated. And, if living in two worlds is the natural state of the developed human being, it nevertheless imposes a responsibility to maintain a balance between inner and outer reality.

If one can stay in the middle, know one is human, relate to both the god and the animal of the god, one is all right. One must remember, over the animal is the god, with the god is the god's animal.[39]

HEALER AT WORK

Jung approached the 1930s with this definition of himself in response to an anonymous woman who had made a portrait of him:

There is some likeness in the upper story but the ensemble is not satisfactory.... My exterior is in strange contrast to my spirit. When I am dead nobody will think that this is the corpse of one with spiritual aspirations. I am the clash of opposites. That makes it frightfully difficult to get me right.[40]

That human range can be seen in everything Jung did, including his therapy work. In reckoning the effectiveness of his treatments with patients, he reported one third really cured, one third considerably improved, and one third not essentially influenced although, even then, post-treatment results could show years later. Jane Wheelwright recounted her initial meeting with Jung as his patient.

"So you're in the soup too," had been one of Jung's opening

Portrait of Jung; drawing by Peter Birkhäusen, 1958. In this portrait, Jung's solidly earthy strength and seeking spirit are apparent. He declared himself to be a "clash of opposites."

Coffin of Khnumnakht; painted wood, Twelfth Dynasty (*c.* 1991–1786 BCE), Egypt.
Horus, whose right eye is the sun and left eye the moon, heals the very earth with his penetrating vision. Born of a loving goddess and a dismembered and resurrected father, it is he who serves humanity. For Jung, "only the wounded physician heals," and then only to the extent that he has healed himself.

remarks – (he loved American slang)....

In my first appointment ... he asked me what my attitude toward him was. I said he would be a catalyst for me. I had read Jung and I was painfully aware of the people around him who had become hopelessly enmeshed in his aura and who seemed to have lost their identity in the sticky, gluey substance of the transference. I was bound not to be one of these. He agreed with me that would be his role. But not long afterwards I heard him say in a gently pleading way from deep down in his humanity, "Can't you see me as a human being?" It was then my objectivity collapsed. I would let myself in for whatever would happen, and the give-and-take between us was launched. Needless to say, the analysis in the long run established that new attitude and new insight and sense of myself that has remained the core of my being to this day. It also convinced me of the importance of a real relationship in the analytical hour. Outside of his study Jung was formal and polite.[41]

He saw his role as doctor in terms not usual for his time.

> When important matters are at stake, it makes all the difference
> whether the doctor sees himself as a part of the drama, or cloaks
> himself in his authority.[42]

> I learned ... [at Burghölzli] that only the physician who feels
> himself deeply affected by his patients could heal. It works only
> when the doctor speaks out of the center of his own psyche, so
> provisionally called "normal," to the sick psyche before him that
> he can hope to heal....
> In the end, only the wounded physician heals and even he, in
> the last analysis, cannot heal beyond the extent to which he has
> healed himself.[43]

Jung sat opposite his patients in direct communication as one human being
to another. Words – and their underlying hinterland, body language and dreams
– were the fishing nets of the personal story. Once brought up for air, shared,
and treated, however unorthodoxly, the contents were inevitably returned to the
individual as a precious possession best understood personally.

> Nothing worse could
> happen to one than to be
> completely understood....
> One would be instantly
> deprived of one's personal *raison
> d'être* if one were. I'd hate it myself....
> Understanding is ... at times a
> veritable murder of the soul as soon
> as it flattens out vitally important
> differences. The core of the
> individual is a mystery of life which
> is snuffed out when it is "grasped."[44]

Eskimo Shaman; stone carving by Lucassie Ohaytook,
1966.
A shamanic healer can embody both disease and cure
for the patient. His ability to jump across all boundaries –
of time, space, and being – at once is his healing gift.

Sometimes Jung's methods were reminiscent of shamanic practice, as Jane Wheelwright told it.

Jung's concrete approach, emphasizing so vividly the reality of the psyche, is what impressed.... My experience of Jung's concrete approach, apart from presenting himself as a person, not a doctor, came in an incident early in the analysis. I had confessed to Jung I feared insanity, a common feeling when one is close to the collective. It had been a secret fear. He made a grab in the air toward me with both hands as if catching a football and then hugging it to himself said "Now I have it and you will not fear any longer."

As I remember it the fear disappeared at that moment.[45]

Aniela Jaffé included this unusual doctor/patient encounter in her book *From the Life and Work of C.G. Jung*:

Once a simple young girl was shown into his consulting room, a schoolteacher from a village.... A doctor, personally unknown to Jung, had sent her to him. She suffered from almost total insomnia and was one of those people who agonize over having done nothing properly and not having met satisfactorily the demands of daily life. What she needed was relaxing. Jung tried to explain this to her, and told her that he himself found relaxation by sailing on the lake, letting himself go with the wind. But he could see from her eyes that she didn't understand. This saddened him, because he wanted to help her, and there was only this single consultation to do it in.

"Then," said Jung, "as I talked of sailing and of the wind, I heard the voice of my mother singing a lullaby to my little sister as she used to do when I was eight or nine, a story of a little girl in a little boat, on the Rhine, with little fishes. And I began, almost without doing it on purpose, to hum what I was telling her about the wind, the waves, the sailing, and relaxation, to the tune of the little lullaby. I hummed those sensations, and I could see that she was 'enchanted.'"

The consultation came to an end, and Jung had to send the girl away. Two years later, at a congress, he met the doctor who had sent her to him. The doctor pressed Jung to tell him what

Detail from *Young Woman in Garden*; oil painting by Mary Cassatt, *c.* 1886.
Jung's intuition could lead him into unusual methods of healing, sometimes very simple in form. He cured a young village girl of insomnia in one consultation by spontaneously humming to her a lullaby about nature that he remembered his mother singing to his sister when he was a boy.

kind of therapy he had used, because, he said, the insomnia had completely disappeared after the girl's visit to Küsnacht and had never come back again.... Naturally Jung was rather embarrassed.

"How was I to explain to him that I had simply listened to something within myself? I had been quite at sea. How was I to tell him that I had sung her a lullaby with my mother's voice? Enchantment like that is the oldest form of medicine."[46]

At a European conference in the 1930s, where Jung's "earthy matter-of-factness" and "at the same time somewhat Mephistophelian effect" on the gathering had been noted, he fielded some rather pious questions about his "mission" and "who his client really was" in distinctly no-nonsense style.

Medicinal Flora; painting by Paul Klee, 1924.
The healer has many natural methods at his disposal including the herbalist's art and his own inner store of being. Each can be potent medicine. Imagination, memory, and the beauty of the earth can all evoke the breath of life.

I am Herr Jung and nobody else, and there is Miss so-and-so. It would not be nice at all if I could not treat such sick people. Besides, I have a certain zest for work. I am enterprising; I have a pioneering spirit. If any kind of screwball at all comes to the door, the explorer in me is awakened, my curiosity, my spirit of adventure, my sympathy. It touches my heart, which is too soft – and people my size usually have something of this; they try to conceal it, but like fools they don't succeed – and I enjoy seeing what can be done with such a crazy fellow. I have made a game out of healing even difficult cases. This is simply a kind of curiosity and sense of adventure....

I can tell you this: When you have to exhaust yourself terribly for a person and you don't get paid for it, in time you lose your taste for it. So I confront the patient as a completely ordinary person, with all his pros and cons.[47]

Stories of Jung's interaction with his patients range from human solicitude to "Go away, you bore me." Jane Wheelwright observed the opposites in Jung at work.

At times Jung's concern for the individual was touching. It did not matter of what color, class, condition the person was, nor how educated. It did not matter from where he came if he was true to himself and sincere in his own quest.

I remember Jung's excitement when a clerk from some humble office from our anonymous Midwest, having saved up enough money, got himself to Zürich to see Jung. He had questions about Jung's writings and he needed to know more. Jung gave him an appointment immediately and at a time when he had already been turning people away for lack of time. He obviously admired this little man and wanted to honor him. Perhaps he had found another loner with courage and independence and determination even though on a humble level? It was a sight to see this great man so touched and flattered and happy that so little a man had sought him out. On other occasions Jung could be harsh, and, at times, it seemed, heartless. He may have had his legitimate reasons, but it was hard to know. There was, for instance, a woman who had been analyzing for years in preparation for analysis with him. The day came when he would take her on. She was overcome in anticipation or by his presence.

For whatever reason, she melted into tears. This went on for every appointment for a considerable length of time. He coped with her dissolved state by reading the newspaper....

Still another woman I knew told me she went to an enormous effort to write a play as homework for her analysis. She finally proudly presented it to him. He handed it back without reading it. He must have rebelled at her slavish effort to please him. And as far as I know she never wrote again.[48]

If Jung didn't understand a patient's dreams, or if he thought they'd be better off with a Freudian or Adlerian approach, he referred them elsewhere. He told Jane Wheelwright's husband Joseph that nobody had "the whole truth" – Freud, Adler, or Jung: "We each have our own truth." The relative validity of both Freud's pleasure principle and Adler's power principle he acknowledged while recognizing that neither exhausted the full expression of psychic wholeness. Many "so-called neurotics" were "divided against themselves" because of the onesidedness of the society they lived in, becoming what he called "optional neurotics."

Pigeon's Egg Head Going to and Returning from Washington; oil painting by George Catlin, 1837–1839.

Some so-called neurotics are divided against themselves, not because of any deep emotional problem, but because modern society imposes a straitjacket of thought and feeling, and confines to one dimension those who would naturally live in two worlds. Whether they were "optional neurotics" or those with "a primitive and modern split," Jung sought to connect them to a deeper, more authentic sense of themselves.

If they had lived in a period and in a milieu in which man was still linked by myth with the world of the ancestors, and thus with nature truly experienced and not merely seen from outside, they would have been spared this division within themselves. I am speaking of those who cannot tolerate the loss of myth and who neither find a way to a merely exterior world as seen by science, nor rest satisfied with an intellectual juggling with words, which has nothing whatever to do with wisdom … their apparent morbidity drops away the moment the gulf between the ego and the unconscious is closed.[49]

Jane Wheelwright counted herself "fortunate" in having the "primitive and modern split" that Jung was interested in studying in 1935, especially as it manifested in people in the second half of life, where he himself was.

Mine had been caused by an identification with nature in a wilderness area … where not even an Indian culture survived to mitigate its potency. On top of this I was sent to sophisticated schools and colleges as my introduction to civilization. Somehow I felt I must make a quantum leap from the social level of Stone Age woman to the twentieth century and Jung could help me. It was sheer luck that I appeared on his doorstep in that phase of his life.

Jung was definitely the patriarch and was paternalistic. His very physical dimension promoted such a role. But I feel, because of his discovery of his anima and his enormous popularity with women, as well as getting support for his new radical ideas from them, especially American women, he, at least theoretically, wanted women to improve their lot and make their legitimate way into the professions. He was not, however, altogether convincing in his behavior. When I encountered him about the first appointment he said he would discuss the time and day with my husband. I said, "What about me?" with the usual American indignation. He said rather clumsily, "That will come later." I give this episode only because it shows him in his spontaneity referring to the man as the controller of a woman's fate. But because of my work with him and the momentum it engendered, I found in the long run my true female independence. Besides, I could also, finally, thanks to him, outgrow my total dependence on his ideas and develop some of my own....

Entwined Buddha; photograph by Linda Connor, Ayuthaya, Thailand, 1988.
The face of Buddha, firmly entwined with visible roots. Buddha is said to have attained enlightenment at the foot of the Bodhi Tree.

Detail from *Sixteen Lohans*; handscroll by Wu Pin, China, Ming Dynasty, c. 1583–1626.
The man who has mastered himself can, by balancing on the law of dharma, walk on water –
that is, he can see above the churning of his unconscious. To be truly an individual, we have
to be prepared to meet life with the confidence and surety that it will teach real lessons.
Growth is work; our tool is our own unflinching ability to see the truth about ourselves that
comes from within and forges hard-won equanimity.

Jung's broad vision did ... constellate for me specifically my
need to strive toward being a free modern woman with my roots
planted deeply in the soil of archaic woman.[50]

Helping people to independence of his authority by reaching inside to their
own was the essence of the work.

I consider it my task and duty to educate my patients and pupils
to the point where they can accept the direct demand that is

made upon them from within....[51]

There is a reasonable amount of certainty that we can show a person what there is, but we cannot hand out the thing which he ought to do....

There would be no difficulty in life if one always knew beforehand how to do a thing. Life is some sort of art and not a straight rail or a ready-made product to be had at every corner....

Nobody can live it for you or instead of you. Your life is what you try to live. If I should try to put you through something it would be my life and not yours.[52]

If you want to go your individual way it is the way you make for yourself, which is never prescribed, which you do not know in advance, and which simply comes into being of itself when you put one foot in front of the other. If you always do the next thing that needs to be done, you will go most safely and surefootedly along the path prescribed by your unconscious.[53]

In her final session with Jung, social activist Isabelle Hamilton Rey was told to "Go home and live it now." As she wrote to her husband,

I did what I came here to do – touch the hem of Dr. Jung's psychological skirt – but it all seems so different now; I think I looked for a sort of spiritual baptism, which would insure protection and perfect understanding; instead it seems to me I have undertaken the tremendous responsibility of maintaining a standard of consciousness which is most difficult. I can never turn back, but God knows the prospect ahead isn't easy either.[54]

As Jung told Alan Watts, he was glad he wasn't a Jungian. "I'm C.G. Jung."

I do not want anyone to be a Jungian.... I want people above all to be themselves.... Should I be found one day only to have created another "ism" then I will have failed in all I tried to do.[55]

HELPERS:
EMMA, TONI

Some of Jung's patients went on to become lifelong friends and to help carry his ideas to the world. Some became analysts themselves. In Zürich, two of the people he recommended patients to as analysts were "either my wife or Frl. T. Wolff."[56]

Emma also helped to develop the anima/animus aspect of the individuation process. Jung encouraged her to learn Latin and Greek, which he himself read with ease, to help her studies. Her research into the Holy Grail legend later became a book completed by Marie-Louise von Franz, herself a one-time patient who became an analyst and foremost world authority on Jungian ideas.

Emma was the first president of the Psychological Club when it was founded in 1916 as a lecture venue *cum* library *cum* social meeting place for analysts, patients, and pupils. Later, when the C.G. Jung Institute was opened, she taught there.

Author Sallie Nichols was one of her students.

I didn't work analytically with Mrs. Jung, and I didn't know her personally, but I did attend her excellent course on the Grail Legend. Each class ended with a brief question period, and I had always observed and admired the simple yet knowledgeable way Mrs. Jung fielded all questions from the most erudite and challenging ones to those that were more pedantic, or even naïve.

But, one day something very unusual happened. Someone raised what appeared to be a very elementary question of fact, to which I assumed Mrs. Jung would respond briefly, but courteously as always. However, on this occasion she

Emma Jung in her study at home in Küsnacht.

As well as becoming an analyst, Mrs. Jung helped develop the anima/animus aspect of the individuation process and did extensive independent work on the Holy Grail legend, which later became a book.

did not answer the question at all! There was a silence. Then she said quite simply, "I don't know the answer to that. I just never thought of this question before!"

I was absolutely dumbfounded! Here sat one of the greatest living authorities on the Grail Legend, the wife of "the" C.G. Jung, if you please, teaching a course at the august C.G. Jung Institute in Zürich and she was perfectly willing to sit there and admit that she not only didn't know the answer to this relatively simple question, but that the question itself had never occurred to her! ...

In the midst of my concern for Mrs. Jung's supposed embarrassment, I suddenly realized that the "embarrassment" was entirely my own! Mrs. Jung, far from feeling embarrassed, humiliated, chagrined, guilty, ignorant, or anything of the sort, was enjoying the situation immensely! She was laughing in the most spontaneous and free way imaginable....

The seminar ended that day with all of us joining Mrs. Jung in her laughter.[57]

Jung at first discouraged Toni Wolff from becoming an analyst because he thought her literary gifts as lyric poet would be overshadowed. It would appear as if, indeed, she didn't fully develop that gift and never sought publication of what she did write. She did become an analyst and assistant to Jung, pioneering new psychological ground in her own right with her analysis of female typology. As president of the Psychological Club for two decades, the outwardly stern, inwardly hypersensitive Toni steered the club through its most flourishing years. Sallie Nichols was in analysis with her.

I worked with Miss Wolff for over a year....

Although she was not a tall woman, she gave me that impression, sitting ramrod straight behind her desk in what I remember as a rather high-backed chair....

But despite her aristocratic bearing and her impeccably tailored clothes, Miss Wolff was one of the most down-to-earth practical human beings I've ever known. Her quiet empathy with the most common human dilemmas and her no-nonsense reactions were strictly contemporary....

I experienced Miss Wolff as a woman of rare passion, compassion, and wisdom.... I had learned that my husband had

Toni Wolff and Jung at Swansea, UK, 1922.

Toni Wolff became an analyst and an assistant to Jung, pioneering an analysis of female psychology and contributing to his book *Psychological Types*.

embarked upon a romance with a European woman.... Way down deep I didn't honestly believe that I and my three "innocent" progeny were about to be tossed out into the snow forever. But the role of Wounded Wife is a tempting one.... So, of course, I went blubbering to Miss Wolff with my woes. She listened attentively and sympathetically to my interminable trials, but when I at last came up for breath, she made a suggestion that still startles me.

"Why don't you ask this other woman to lunch tomorrow?"

"You mean, a wee drop of arsenic in the tea?" I asked, hope of deliverance shining through my tears.

"By no means," replied Miss Wolff sternly. "But, you would then get to know her a bit, you might even like her." Then after a pause, Miss Wolff added this: "You know, sometimes if a man's wife is big enough to leap over the hurdle of self-pity, she may find that her supposed rival has even helped the marriage! This 'other woman' can sometimes help a man live out certain aspects of himself that his wife either can't fulfill, or else doesn't especially want to. As a result, some of the wife's energies are now freed for her own creative interests and development, often with the result that the marriage not only survives, but emerges even stronger than before!"

But I did not follow Miss Wolff's advice.... I preferred nursing my fantasy of my rival as a 'wicked witch' to facing her human reality. Since then, I've often wished I had found the courage to ask her to ... lunch![58]

Detail from group photograph from the Third International Psychoanalytic Congress, Weimar, Germany, 1911.

Front row, second left, Emma Jung; far right, Toni Wolff, representative from Zürich. Second row, far left, Sigmund Freud, representative from Vienna; next right, Carl Jung, representative from Küsnacht. This is one of the few photographs of Jung, Emma, and Toni together.

While Emma and Toni are known to have worked together for a time with a male colleague of Jung's to analyze the complexities of their personal situation, the trio's public lives were readily seen, as noted by author Dr. Joseph Henderson.

Their social relationship ... could be observed by those of us who knew and worked with them analytically during the 1920s and 30s....

A socially prominent couple from New York ... wanted to give a dinner party for C.G., Emma, and Toni before a Chinese Ball, a fancy dress benefit at the Grand Hotel Dolder.... It was a delightful evening ... with everyone in good humor, done up in some form of Chinese coat or mildly disguised with an oriental eye makeup in preparation for the ball....

Jung, true to habit in his own milieu, was full of energy

for making the party a success.... I recall no strain or tension between Emma Jung and Toni Wolff. They seemed perfectly at ease with each other as was Jung with each of them.

At other times in later years I was aware that Jung was careful to give Emma and Toni their affectionate places in his public life. When he came to deliver the Tavistock Lectures in 1935 he brought Toni Wolff as his companion and hostess. I remember the surprise and pleasure of the Englishwomen who met her at her elegance in wearing a different striking hat for each occasion. Two years later in 1937 Jung again came to London to give a public lecture after a trip to America and this time his companion and hostess was Emma Jung who had her own style and dignity.

Fowler McCormick, a businessman and philanthropist from Chicago, was a close friend of the Jung family and he often told me in later years how deeply the Jungs and Toni were respected in their own circle for keeping their personal problems to themselves. Even the Jung children did not know of their father's close relation to Toni until long after it began, even though they often saw her in their home. He felt, and I would corroborate this impression, that as nearly as possible in our monogamous society, Jung found two wives in these women....[59]

Portraits at the Stock Exchange; pastel by Edgar Degas, c. 1879.
Although very unusual for its time, or any time, Jung's relationship with both Emma and Toni was openly known. It had a public face at social gatherings and international lectures as well as its private aspect.

FAMILY LIFE

The five Jung children were brought up along liberal lines, with their father teaching them comparative religions and allowing them their choice of Sunday schools, confirmation, and careers. Playtime with the children was an essential part of holidays and weekends. Before Bollingen there was a vacation island at the upper end of Lake Zürich where natural living was the mode. They lived in tents; firewood came from the forest and water from the lake. Creative games were invented around natural objects of wood, sand, and stone, or played on boats where "Papa" Jung was captain to the children's boatmen.

Jung loved to work with his hands – painting, chiseling, building models of ships – often involving the children's participation while telling them stories that spurred their imagination. Hikes in the forest, sailing, cycling, or working in the garden were also shared with family and a few close friends.

Franz Jung, who once described his father as "maddening and marvelous" helped him build his retreat at Bollingen. In 1928 the Jungs bought their first automobile, a family car they called "Lina," to which Jung added a red two-seater sports car.

Jung's first automobile, c. 1928.

REMINISCENCES

ELIZABETH SHEPLEY SERGEANT – I had seen him often as a highly civilized modernist driving a red Chrysler through the twisting streets of Zürich; pondering the problems of the psyche in his sober booklined study with its Oriental paintings and Christian stained glass ... before I came upon the primitive Jung, one rainy summer day, outside his favorite dwelling place [Bollingen] – a gray stronghold, of medieval outline, standing alone and apart, surrounded by hills and water – where, when his work as a doctor is over, he retires to become for a season the detached scholar and writer who turns experience into theory. Ensconced there in the shelter of the round stone tower which he had built with his own hands, dressed in a bright blue linen overall, with his powerful arms in a tub of water, I beheld Dr. Jung earnestly engaged in washing his blue jeans....

Jung in his study; photograph by Karsh of Ottawa.

Jung's book-lined study was notable for images from many different cultures, East and West, including Christian stained glass windows. This was his place of work, while Bollingen remained his preferred place of inner repose.

Illustration from the *Mutus Liber* (*Mutable Book*), La Rochelle, France, 1677.
A couple kneels in prayer. He is an alchemist; she is the *soror mystica* (sister in the mystery).
Like "an old alchemist," Jung, in his Bollingen kitchen, concocted elaborate dishes from a
variety of ingredients. His guests often felt a touch of magic about their visit.

Dr. Jung never does anything by halves. When he walks
up and down the floor of the Psychological Club, expounding
a dream to his advanced students, every cell and fiber of his
physical being seems to participate; every resource of his great
learning ... and his native wisdom is turned in a single living
stream upon the question in hand. This massive, peaceful man in
blue was putting the same zest and interest into washing. No part
of Jung was left in Küsnacht giving consultations.[60]

Barbara Hannah – Toni paid back hospitality by asking Jung to
invite me to Bollingen. I was frankly terrified when I first arrived
at the Tower. It was very cold weather and Jung was cooking in
his original round kitchen in a long Oriental robe which he often
wore in cold weather. He looked like a picture I had once seen
of an old alchemist at work among his retorts. He looked more
whole than ever…. Toni, who was also staying there, just gave me
some tea and told me to take a chair by the fire and watch Jung
cook, then busied herself with fetching the things he asked for
and her own jobs. Jung was entirely engrossed in some absorbing
cooking and in watching the fire. (He was a most unusually good
cook and used in those days to cook the most complicated dishes.

I remember one sauce with no fewer than sixteen ingredients!) I did not yet know him well enough to feel it as a companionable silence (which I learned later to enjoy more than anything), so after two or three hours I took an opportunity, when he did not seem quite so engrossed, to murmur: "I am scared stiff." Although only a faint amused smile indicated that he had even heard my remark, the ice was broken and I began to feel at home. After a bit he gave me an aperitif … then I even got a small job or two to do, and finally we were ready to sit down at the round table. The marvelous food and wine rapidly banished my fear, though I was fortunate enough still to say nothing, except for a few appreciative gruntlike murmurs while we were eating. That was indeed fortunate because, as I learned later, Jung hated to talk while he was eating a really good meal. (He used to quote his mother, who said that chattering was disrespectful to good food.) The only remark I remember him making during that first meal was: "Oh, well, you already know how to enjoy your food, that is one thing (emphasis on the one!) I shall not have to teach you!"[61]

CHOREOGRAPHER AND POET HELENA HENDERSON – I remember the damp, stony, medieval look and smell of the house, and Dr. Jung sitting by the fireplace with a stocking cap on his head, stirring a stew in a big iron pot. We ate the stew later at a refectory table in another stone-floored room. Dr. Jung gave us a lot of wine and made us all quite drunk in a pleasant way, and all I remember is everyone telling jokes, but not what they were. Only when we had finished our second helping of stew, and might have been ready for another, he asked us to guess what a certain kind of meat in it could be. We guessed heart, lungs and all kinds of unusual things, and finally had to give up. He then revealed that it was dried cow's udder, and after that no one seemed to want any more. Great joke! He threw the rest to the dogs under the table – another medieval gesture.

I remember driving back in a haze of wine and enjoyment. I remember, but find it hard to convey, the fairytale quality of the place and everything that happened there. Above all I remember someone who, by his every word and action, gave one the feeling that life is a good thing – something even more precious to me than anything he put on paper.[62]

Foundation stone, Ascona, Switzerland.
Olga Fröbe-Kapteyn, founder of the Eranos Conferences at Lake Maggiore, erected this stone in homage to the Unknown Spirit of the center. The conferences were begun "to receive the secret of the spirit with reverence..." (*Jahre Eranos*).

ANIELA JAFFÉ – Jung gave free rein to his emotions, both positive and negative, with his friends and in daily life. In his younger years his laughter rang out far and wide like a fanfare. Once there approached on the terrace ... where the Eranos meetings were held every year ... an amiable stranger, no longer young, whom none of the participants knew. He excused himself for intruding and explained why he had come: he wanted to meet the man who was laughing so heartily and uproariously that he, walking alone on the road ... high above Casa Eranos, had irresistibly been infected by it. Naturally Jung was enchanted and instantly engaged the stranger in conversation.[63]

From their inception in 1933, Jung played a leading role in the international and multidisciplinary Eranos Conferences, where for nearly two decades he launched his new ideas. Jung's theories were beginning to be applied to widely divergent disciplines – theology, political science, jurisprudence, and literature. Hermann Hesse adopted Jung's ideas in several novels; so did H.G. Wells, who acknowledged his thinking as "a bright light in my darkness and a gold mine for reflection." Jung himself wrote essays on poetry, literature, and art, including the works of James Joyce and Picasso. Public life also brought a series of lecture tours and honorary doctorates in European, American, English, and Indian universities, as well as the city of Zürich's Prize for Literature.

JANE WHEELWRIGHT – Observing him in Zürich, surrounded by people, it was nevertheless clear he was going it alone. He contained the others, but there was no one to contain him.[64]

Yet Jung confessed in a letter in 1932,

I have attacks of feeling horribly inferior. I have to digest a whole span of life full of mistakes and stupidity. Anyway feelings of inferiority are the counterpart of power. Wanting to be better or more intelligent than one is, is power too. It is difficult enough to be what one is and yet endure oneself and for once forgive one's own sins with Christian charity. That is damnably difficult.[65]

STRIFE

The highly charged years leading up to World War II fanned one of the public controversies that punctuated Jung's life. It included recurring accusations of anti-Semitism and pro-Nazi leanings, which are occasionally echoed even today.

In the early 1930s Jung, like many others, saw political events in Germany as "uncertain" in outcome, with some possibility of a positive result from the upheaval. It was a view he held for about two years. In 1933, at the urgent request of its leading members, Vice President Jung accepted the vacant presidency of the General Medical Society for Psychotherapy and editorship of its publication, the *Zentralblatt*, both located in Germany. This was at a time when Hitler had just come to power and all German institutions stood in danger of being forced to "conform" to Nazi ideology.

Although the Society was international in membership it was dominated by Germans and included many Jews. As a Swiss citizen, Jung could act independently, and did. Within months he rewrote the constitution to enlarge the organization into the International General Society for Psychotherapy, which included a series of national groups with voting rights, thereby precluding any one section having control. It also allowed for individual membership for people not wishing, or unable, to be affiliated with a national group, thus protecting the Jews. Letters show he then sought Swiss, Danish, Swedish, and Dutch help.

Jung with Mathias Heinrich Göering, head of the German section of the International Medical Society for Psychotherapy in 1934.

Jung had accepted the post of Vice President and later the presidency of the General Medical Society, which he almost immediately enlarged into the International General Medical Society.

Dear Colleague....

By means of this organization I am trying to prevent the special political currents in the German group, which is numerically the strongest, from spilling over into the Society as a whole. This is what many foreigners fear, particularly the Jews, who as you know are very numerous. If we succeed in organizing some national groups in neutral countries, this will act as a counterweight and at the same time afford the Germans a much needed opportunity to maintain a connection with the outside world in their present spiritual isolation. This connection is essential for the continued development of psychotherapy in Germany....[66]

The separate German section was "conformed" with Professor Göering, cousin of the Reichsmarschall, as its president. But it was the first issue of the Society's periodical under Jung's name as editor that really ignited the controversy. Jung had agreed to a previously planned special supplement of the *Zentralblatt* for circulation in Germany only. Signed by Göering, the special edition obliged German society members to adopt Hitler's political and ideological principles. By negligence, mistake, or design Göering's Manifesto also appeared in the international *Zentralblatt* without Jung's knowledge and against his orders to its managing editor, Dr. Walter Cimbal, in Germany.

Dear Colleague....

I ... take this opportunity of informing you that the fact that Göering's Manifesto, which should have appeared only in the special German issue, has nevertheless come out in the *Zentralblatt* has displeased me. As you will remember, I told you of my express wish that the German issue should be signed by Prof. Göering. I as a foreigner do not fit into German internal politics. Also, with regard to foreign subscribers, it is a regrettable tactical blunder when purely domestic political manifestos, which can at a pinch be taken as German necessities, are rammed down the throats of foreign readers who are critical enough as it is.... I would ... urgently request you to make the *Zentralblatt* intended for foreign circulation unpolitical in every respect, otherwise it is quite impossible for foreign subscribers to join the Society....

The *Zentralblatt* blunder has already set off a campaign against me in Zürich ... as President of the International Society I must make absolutely sure that the periodical under my direction maintains a scientific form outside all politics.[67]

The same edition carried an editorial by Jung on differences between Jewish and German psychology.

I would like to state expressly that this is not meant to suggest any depreciation of Semitic psychology, any more than a depreciation of that of the Chinese is intended when speaking of the characteristic psychology of the Far East.[68]

An avalanche of public attacks, opened by Dr. Bally in Switzerland, accused Jung of anti-Semitism and Nazi sympathies. Jung stated his position in two articles.

I found myself faced with a moral conflict ... should I as a prudent neutral withdraw on this side of the frontier, live and wash my hands in innocence or should I – as I was well aware – lay myself open to attack and the unavoidable misunderstanding which no one can escape who, out of a higher necessity, has to come

Set design for *Queen of the Night* (from *The Magic Flute*); aquatint by Karl Friedrich Schinkel, Germany, 1819.
By 1933, the dark night of the Third Reich had enveloped Germany. All institutions were under the tight control of the state.

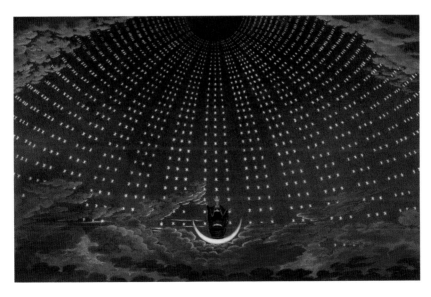

The Jew, etc.; oil and charcoal by R.B. Kitaj, 1976 (unfinished). Although a "neutral" Swiss, Jung was confronted with a moral dilemma by the rise of Nazism: Should he withdraw to a safe distance, or do what he could for international psychiatry and its members in spite of Hitler's Germany?

to terms with the political powers that be in Germany? Should I sacrifice the interests of science, of loyalty to my colleagues, of the friendship which binds me to many German physicians, and the living community of German language and intellectual culture, to my egotistic comfort and different political outlook? ... So I had no alternative but to lend the weight of my name and of my independent position for the benefit of my friends....

The main point is to get a young and insecure science into a position of safety during an earthquake.... Medicine has nothing to do with politics ... and therefore it can and should be practiced for the good of suffering humanity under all governments.... Man after all still has a soul and is not just an ox fatted for political slaughter. If I am called into the arena for the sake of the soul I shall follow the call wherever it may be.... The doctor who, in wartime, gives his help to the wounded of the other side will surely not be held a traitor to his country....

Admittedly I was incautious ... as to do the very thing most open to misunderstanding at the present moment: I tabled the Jewish question ... may it not be asked wherein lie the peculiar differences between Jewish and an essentially Christian outlook? If I were in a position – as Dr. Bally supposes me to be – of not being able to point out a single difference between the two psychologies, it would amount to exactly the same thing as not being able to make plausible the difference between the peculiarities of the English and the Americans, or the French and the Germans.... All branches of mankind unite in one stem, yes, but what is a stem without separate branches?

I have no hesitation in admitting that it is a highly unfortunate and confusing coincidence that my scientific programme should have been superimposed without my co-operation and against my express wish, on a political manifesto.[69]

Inevitably, the old break with Freud was resurrected, now viewed with racist overtones. In addition, some of Jung's statements on Jewish culture were seen to echo the general limited knowledge of it at the time by both gentiles and many Jews. Freud himself, for instance, had once declared himself unaware of any Jewish mystic tradition. Jung's letters give the tenor of the times:

13th April 1934
Dear Frau von Speyer,
I have fallen foul of contemporary history.... People now think I am a blood-boltered anti-Semite because I have helped the German doctors to consolidate their Psychotherapeutic Society and because I have said there are certain differences between

Funeral; woodcut by Solomon Yudovin, 1926. The mass hysteria of the 1930s and 40s would soon lead twenty million people, six million of them Jews, to their deaths, and convulse the entire world in war. It would take an atomic explosion, a new manifestation of the shadow, to end the collective insanity.

Jewish and so-called Aryan psychology which are mainly due to the fact that the Jews have a cultural history that is 2,000 years older than the so-called Aryan. There has been a terrific shindy over this. It is no pleasure to be well known. You are then like a city on a mountain and cannot remain hidden.[70]

Dear Dr. Cohen,
I would like to thank you for your understanding and decent article in the *Israelitisches Wochenblatt*. Such an event at a time like this, when stupidity is celebrating veritable orgies, is a rarity.

Your criticism of my lack of knowledge in things Jewish is quite justified. I don't understand Hebrew. But you seem to impute a political attitude to me which in reality I do not possess. I am absolutely not an opponent of the Jews even though I am an opponent of Freud's. I criticize him because of his materialistic and intellectualistic and – last but not least – irreligious attitude and not because he is a Jew....

My relation with Germany is very recent and is due to idiotic altruism and not at all to political sentiment.[71]

My dear Kirsch....
You ought to know me sufficiently well to realize that an unindividual stupidity like anti-Semitism cannot be laid at my door. You know well enough how very much I take the human being as a personality and how I continually endeavor to lift him out of his collective condition and make him an individual. This, as you know, is possible only if he acknowledges his peculiarity which has been forced on him by fate. No one who is a Jew can become a human being without knowing that he is a Jew, since this is the basis from which he can reach out toward a higher humanity. This holds good for all nations and races. Nationalism – disagreeable as it is – is therefore a *sine qua non*, but the individual must not remain stuck in it....[72]

My dear Murray....
I don't think that I have paranoic delusions about persecution. The difficulty is very real. Whatever I touch and wherever I go I meet with this prejudice that I'm a Nazi and that I'm in close affiliation with the German government. I had very real proof of

this and corresponding difficulties this summer in England. Even in India I discovered that a faked photograph with my name had been sent to scientific societies … from Vienna. On this photo, which I possess, I'm represented as a Jew of the particularly vicious kind. Such experiences are no delusions.[73]

Letters, publications, and statements by prominent Jewish supporters now show that Jung in the 1930s and 40s helped countless individual Jews with advice and assistance to safety in England and America. As well as offering active support professionally, Jung included an essay by a Jewish author in one of his own books and wrote a foreword to a book by his Jewish pupil Gerhard Adler. Nonetheless, there is criticism of the timing and accuracy of his remarks on Jewish psychology and culture in a period of racial fanaticism on one side and hypersensitivity and danger to life on the other.

Jung also staunchly supported the speaking rights of Jewish members of the Society against German pressure, and finally resigned in 1939 because he couldn't get a guarantee from the German section and its new allies that the organization would continue without discrimination on "so-called Aryan" lines. By that time, Jung had walked out of a summoned meeting in Goebbels' office and later made increasingly hostile statements about the Nazi regime. In a letter, he wrote, "On account of my critical utterances I was 'marked down' by the Gestapo, my books were banned in Germany and in France they were for the most part destroyed."[74] At one point, when his name was discovered on the Nazi blacklist, he had to make a sudden exit from his Zürich home to safety in the mountains on the advice of top Swiss Army authorities.[75]

28th September 1939
Dear Dr. Harding.…
We naturally hope not to be implicated in the war, but there is only one conviction in Switzerland, that if it has to be, it will be on the side of the Allies. There is no doubt and no hesitation; the unanimous conviction in Switzerland is that Germany has lost her national honor to an unspeakable degree, and the Germans in as much as they still think know it too.…[76]

Five days before that letter was written, Freud died in exile in London. Two years before, his safe arrival in England from Nazi Vienna prompted a telegram of congratulations from Jung, the only personal contact between the two men since their break. Friends of both Freud and Jung have testified that neither man ever fully healed the wounded feelings of that friendship's end.

INDIAN SUMMER

Before the war hit there was an Indian summer, literally, for Jung – the last of his cultural expeditions, this one at the invitation of the British Indian Government in 1937. He had already published a psychological commentary on *The Tibetan Book of the Dead*, had given the Terry Lectures at Yale University on "Psychology and Religion," and had "read a great deal about Indian philosophy and religious history," which left him "deeply convinced of the value of Oriental wisdom."

In India I was principally concerned with the question of the psychological nature of evil. I had been very much impressed by the way this problem is integrated in Indian spiritual life....

I saw that Indian spirituality contains as much of evil as of good. The Christian strives for good and succumbs to evil; the Indian feels himself to be outside good and evil, and seeks to realize this state by meditation or yoga. My objection is that, given such an attitude, neither good nor evil takes on any real outline, and this produces a certain stasis. One does not really believe in evil, and one does not really believe in good....

The Indian's goal is not moral perfection, but the condition of *nirvana* [liberation from the opposites and the ten thousand things]. He wishes to free himself from nature; in keeping with this aim, he seeks in meditation the condition of imagelessness and emptiness. I, on the other hand, wish to persist in the state of lively contemplation of nature and of the psychic images. I want to be freed neither from human beings, nor from myself, nor from nature; for all these appear to me the greatest of miracles. Nature, the psyche, and life appear to me like divinity unfolded – and what more could I wish for? To me the supreme meaning of Being can consist only in the fact that it *is*, not that it is not or is no longer....

Real liberation becomes possible for me only when I have done all that I was able to do.... If I withdraw from participation, I am virtually amputating the corresponding part of my psyche....

A man who has not passed through the inferno of his passions has never overcome them.... Whenever we give up, leave behind, and forget too much, there is always the danger that the things we have neglected will return with added force.[77]

Devi Drinking from a Skull Cup; painting, Punjab, India, c. 1660–1670.
A seventeenth-century devotional shows opposite forms of the goddess: blessed Lakshmi attended by darkly terrifying Kali. On the back of the image is written in Sanskrit, "One should meditate … in the lotus of Lakshmi's heart on … [the] goddess of remembrance." For the Hindu, the goddesses are not in opposition, for they both serve the Godhead.

Jung observed that in "the dreamlike world of India life has not withdrawn into the capsule of the head. It is still the whole body that lives." On a visit to the Black Pagoda of Konarak he encountered the way India includes sexuality in its religion in a manner quite foreign to the West.

The pagoda is covered from base to pinnacle with exquisitely obscene sculptures … which he [a pandit] explained to me as a means to achieve spiritualization. I objected – pointing to a group of young peasants who were standing open-mouthed before the monument admiring these splendors – that such young men were scarcely undergoing spiritualization at the moment, but were

Carved stone frieze,
Devi Jagadambú Temple,
Khajuraho, India, c. 1600.
Sexual ecstasy is portrayed
in sculpture on the "heaven
bands" of the temple at
Khajuraho to remind us of
dharma (law) and lead us to
enlightenment.

much more likely having their heads filled with sexual fantasies.
Whereupon he replied, "But that is just the point. How can they
ever become spiritualized if they do not first fulfill their karma?
These admittedly obscene images are here for the very purpose
of recalling to the people their dharma [law]; otherwise these
unconscious fellows might forget it."[78]

If you want to learn the greatest lesson India can teach you,
wrap yourself in the cloak of your moral superiority, go to the
Black Pagoda of Konarak, sit down in the shadow of the mighty
ruin that is still covered with the most amazing collection of
obscenities, read Murray's cunning *Handbook of India*, which
tells you how to be properly shocked by this lamentable state of
affairs ... and then analyze carefully and with the utmost honesty
all your reactions, feelings, and thoughts. It will take you quite a
while, but in the end ... you will have learned something about
yourself, and about the white man in general, which you have
probably never heard of from anyone else ... a trip to India is
on the whole most edifying and, from a psychological point of
view, most advisable, although it may give you considerable
headaches.[79]

While in this "alien, highly differentiated culture" Jung had one of his characteristic big dreams that revealed a sense of direction for him. The dreamer found himself with a number of Zürich friends on an island off the coast of southern England. Before them was a castle dimly lit by candles, which he recognized as the home of the Holy Grail. But the Grail wasn't there yet. Jung knew it was their task to bring the Grail to the castle from the small, uninhabited, and solitary house on the island where it was hidden. Next he found himself on the shoreline of a deserted, desolate area. With neither bridge nor boat to be seen he realized he would have to swim across alone to fetch the Grail.

Imperiously, the dream wiped away all the intense impressions of India and swept me back to the too-long-neglected concerns of the Occident, which had formerly been expressed in the quest for the Holy Grail as well as the search for the philosopher's stone. I was taken out of the world of India, and reminded that India was not my task, but only a part of the way – admittedly a significant one – which should carry me closer to my goal. It was as though the dream were asking me, "What are you doing in India? Rather seek for yourself and your fellows the healing vessel, the *salvator mundi*, which you urgently need. For your state is perilous; you are all in imminent danger of destroying all that centuries have built up."[80]

The Alchemist; detail of manuscript page from Salomon Trismosin, *Splendor Solis*, 1582.
The philosopher carries the healing vessel to save the world (*salvator mundi*).

PART THREE

OF THE SOUL

PAGE 150: *Apparition*; detail of painting by Odilon Redon, 1910.

ABOVE: *Seed*; painting by Francesco Clemente, 1990.

It is quite possible that we look at the world from the wrong side and that we might find the right answer by changing our point of view and looking at it from the other side, that is, not from outside, but from inside.[1]

VISIONS

Jung used the war years in neutral Switzerland to further his alchemical and religious studies. If isolation from the international scene and rationing of food and gasoline kept outer life curtailed, inner experience deepened.

One night I awoke and saw, bathed in bright light at the foot of my bed, the figure of Christ on the Cross. It was not quite life-size, but extremely distinct; and I saw that his body was made of greenish gold. The vision was marvelously beautiful, and yet I was profoundly shaken by it....

The green gold is the living quality which the alchemists saw not only in man but also in inorganic nature. It is an expression of the life-spirit ... the Anthropos who animates the whole cosmos.... This spirit has poured himself out into everything, even into inorganic matter; he is present in metal and stone. My vision was thus a union of the Christ-image with his analogue in matter, the *filius macrocosmi*.[2]

Jung told Barbara Hannah of another unsettling experience.

When news of the unholy alliance of Germany with Russia burst upon a horrified Europe, Jung was further disturbed by a most indigestible dream ... that Hitler was "the devil's Christ," the anti-Christ, but that nevertheless, as such, he was the instrument of God. He told me it took him a long time and much effort before he was able to accept this idea.[3]

That added to a "visionary dream"

Green Death; painting by Odilon Redon, c. 1905.
According to Jung, green gold is the color that the alchemists saw as an expression of the life-spirit permeating man and matter.

Woodcut of the comet of 1299 from *Liber Chronicarum Mundi*, Nuremberg, 1493. Jung experienced dreams of cataclysm. After the end of World War I, he had prescient intimations of the impending crises that would explode by 1940, as the world entered the Age of Aquarius.

which had haunted him since 1918 following the peace declaration of World War I.

I was returning to Switzerland from a trip in Germany. My body was covered with burns and my clothes were burnt full of holes, for I had seen fire falling like rain from heaven and consuming the cities of Germany. I had an intimation that the crucial year would be 1940.[4]

To Peter Bayne, his close friend in England, Jung wrote in 1940,

My Dear Peter,
This is the fateful year for which I have waited more than twenty-five years. I did not know that it was such a disaster. Although since 1918 I knew that a terrible fire would spread over Europe beginning in the North East, I have no vision beyond 1940 concerning the fate of Europe. This year reminds me of the enormous earthquake in 26 B.C. that shook down the great temple of Karnak. It was the prelude to the destruction of all temples, because a new time had begun. 1940 is the year when we approach the meridian of the first star in Aquarius. It is the premonitory earthquake of the New Age....
   It is difficult to be old in these days. One is helpless. On the other hand one feels happily estranged from this world. I like nature but not the world of man or the world to be....
   In autumn I resume my lectures ... about the individuation process in the Middle Ages! That's the only thing with me one could call up to date. I loathe the new style, the new Art, the new Music, Literature, Politics, and above all the new Man. It's the old beast that has not changed since the troglodytes.
   My dear Peter, I am with you and with old England![5]

In 1944 Jung, aged sixty-nine, had a heart attack which kept him at death's door for several weeks while his interior life produced a series of visions.

It seemed to me that I was high up in space. Far below I saw the globe of the earth, bathed in a gloriously blue light. I saw the deep blue sea and the continents....

The sight of the earth from this height was the most glorious thing I had ever seen.

After contemplating it for a while, I turned around.... A short distance away I saw in space a tremendous dark block of stone, like a meteorite. It was about the size of my house, or even bigger. It was floating in space, and I myself was floating in space....

An entrance led into a small antechamber. To the right of the entrance, a black Hindu sat silently in lotus posture upon a stone

Seated Jain; marble, Tirhankara, India.
Following a severe heart attack at the age of sixty-nine, Jung's interior life became even more vivid. In one of a series of visions, he encountered a seated yogi in meditation, who pointed the way to self-knowledge.

bench. He wore a white gown, and I knew that he expected me....

As I approached the steps leading up to the entrance into the rock, a strange thing happened: I had the feeling that everything was being sloughed away; everything I aimed at or wished for or thought, the whole phantasmagoria of earthly existence, fell away or was stripped from me – an extremely painful process. Nevertheless something remained; it was as if I now carried along with me everything I had ever experienced or done, everything that had happened around me. I might also say: it was with me, and I was it....

This experience gave me a feeling of extreme poverty, but at the same time of great fullness. There was no longer anything I wanted or desired. I existed in an objective form; I was what I had been and lived. At first the sense of annihilation predominated, of having been stripped or pillaged; but suddenly that became of no consequence....

Something else engaged my attention: as I approached the temple I had the certainty that I was about to enter an illuminated room and would meet there all those people to whom I belong in reality. There I would at last understand – this too was a certainty – what historical nexus I or my life fitted into. I would know what had been before me, why I had come into being, and where my life was flowing. My life as I lived it had often seemed to me like a story that has no beginning and no end ... many questions had remained unanswered. Why had it taken this course? Why had I brought these particular assumptions with me? What had I made of them? What will follow? I felt sure that I would receive an answer to all these questions as soon as I entered the rock temple....

While I was thinking over these matters ... from the direction of Europe, an image floated up. It was my doctor, Dr. H. – or, rather, his likeness – framed by a golden chain or a golden laurel wreath. I knew at once ... "he is coming in his primal form...."

As he stood before me, a mute exchange of thought took place between us. Dr. H. had been delegated by the earth to deliver a message to me, to tell me that there was a protest against my going away. I had no right to leave the earth and must return. The moment I heard that, the vision ceased.

I was profoundly disappointed, for now it all seemed to have

The Accused; charcoal on paper by Odilon Redon, 1886.
After his brush with death in 1944, Jung was slow to recover. "I could not eat .... Life and the whole world struck me as a prison."

been for nothing....

In reality, a good three weeks were still to pass before I could truly make up my mind to live again. I could not eat because all food repelled me.... Life and the whole world struck me as a prison....

During those weeks I lived in a strange rhythm. By day I was usually depressed.... Gloomily, I thought, "Now I must go back to this drab world." Toward evening I would fall asleep, and my sleep would last until about midnight. Then I would come to myself and lie awake for about an hour, but in an utterly transformed state. It was as if I were in an ecstasy. I felt as though I were floating in space, as though I were safe in the womb of the universe – in a tremendous void, but filled with the highest possible feeling of happiness. "This is eternal bliss," I thought. "This cannot be described; it is far too wonderful!"

Everything around me seemed enchanted.... I myself was, so it seemed, in the ... garden of pomegranates, and the wedding of Tifereth with Malchuth was taking place. Or else I was Rabbi Simon ben Jochai, whose wedding in the afterlife was being celebrated. It was the mystic marriage as it appears in the Kabbalistic tradition.... At bottom it was I myself: I was the marriage....

Gradually the garden of pomegranates faded away and changed. There followed the Marriage of the Lamb, in a Jerusalem festively bedecked.... There were ineffable states of joy. Angels were present, and light. I myself was the "Marriage of the Lamb."

That, too, vanished, and there came a new image, the last vision. I walked up a wide valley to the end ... a classical amphitheater ... magnificently situated in the green landscape. And there, in this theater, the *hierosgamos* was being celebrated. Men and women dancers came onstage, and upon a flower-decked couch All-father Zeus and Hera consummated the mystic marriage, as it is described in the *Iliad*.

All these experiences were glorious ... so fantastically beautiful that by comparison this world appeared downright ridiculous. As I approached closer to life again, they grew fainter, and scarcely three weeks after the first vision they ceased altogether....

We shy away from the word "eternal," but I can describe the experience only as the ecstasy of a non-temporal state in which present, past, and future are one. Everything that happens in time had been brought together into a concrete whole. Nothing was distributed over time, nothing could be measured by temporal concepts. The experience might best be defined as a state of feeling, but one which cannot be produced by imagination.... One is interwoven into an indescribable whole and yet observes

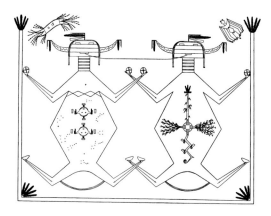

Outline of sandpainting of Navajo cosmic couple, used in the Shooting Chant. A Navajo Indian version of the *hierosgamos*, the mystic wedding. Here the sky is united with earth, helping to keep the world in balance. Navajo sandpainting was used by shamans in traditional chants to heal both bodies and spirits.

Wandjina Aboriginal Australian rock art. This is one of the oldest iconic images known to man. Shamans of indigenous cultures worldwide, through an arduous journey of dismemberment and self-renewal, experience inner psychic forces and work with them to heal others.

it with complete objectivity.[6]

The dissolution of our timebound form in eternity brings no loss of meaning. Rather does the little finger know itself a member of the hand.[7]

As Barbara Hannah recounts:

There was also a vision or experience – not mentioned in *Memories* – which he described to Emma Jung and myself very vividly, when I visited him in the hospital during his early convalescence … he told us then that as he was recovering from the very worst of his illness, he felt that his body had been dismembered and cut up into small pieces. Then, over quite a long period, it was slowly collected and put together again with the greatest care. This is a very interesting parallel to the widespread primitive rituals that were experienced by shamans or medicine men. There are innumerable such examples all over the world, described by Mircea Eliade in his … book on shamanism. For example, both in Siberia and Australia the candidate for shamanism "is subjected to an operation by semi-divine beings or ancestors, in which his body is dismembered and his internal organs and bones are renewed…. Very frequently crystals or other symbolic stones are introduced into the renewed body. I remember Jung saying that day that he had been obliged to do most of or all the reassembling himself, so it is interesting that Eliade wrote: "The primitive magician, the medicine man or shaman is not only a sick man, he is above all a sick man who has been cured, who has succeeded in curing himself."[8]

REMINISCENCES
POST-WAR

D Day – the beginning of the end of World War II – arrived while Jung was still in hospital recovering from his heart attack.

Our so-called peace is a troubled affair and the greatest part of Europe is still in hysterics. No wonder really! The mental and moral, social and financial catastrophe is simply gigantic. The mental and moral devastation is the one I'm chiefly concerned with, since we begin now to get more immediate and personal acquaintance with the facts of the atrocities of the war....

I must say that before the Hitler era I still had some illusions which have been radically destroyed by the prodigious efforts of the Germans. I really had not thought that man could be so absolutely bad. I thought he could be evil, but evil has at least a certain character, while evil in Germany was rotten. It was a carrion of evil, unimaginably worse than the normal devil. Since Germany is not on the moon, I have drawn my conclusions for the rest of mankind.[9]

In 1946, Jung was invited by the University of Zürich to a dinner in honor of Winston Churchill.

22nd September, 1946
Permit me to thank you and the University once again for the invitation to Winston Churchill's reception and quite particularly for the honor of seating me next to the illustrious guest. Conversation with him, however, made no small demands on one's

Woodcut of a demon, medieval.
As the war came to an end, Jung became more aware of the devastating evil wreaked on Europe by Hitler. He felt his illusions of living in a civilized world were utterly destroyed by knowledge of man's apparently bottomless inhumanity.

tact and ingenuity, as I was constantly in doubt as to how much question and answer I might expect from that very tired man. Nevertheless I thank you for one of the most interesting experiences of my life.[10]

Dear Dr. Jacobi....
Your news that Churchill was not bored at our table was a great relief. Conversation with him was no easy matter since he directed his answers mostly to the House of Commons....
P.S. I nearly fell over with astonishment when I discovered that I had been seated next to Churchill – and at a University dinner too! "There will be signs and wonders...."[11]

On both occasions when the two men met, it was by Churchill's request that they were seated together, largely because of his daughter Mary's interest in Jung's work.

It was in the post-war years that Miss A.I. Allenby first wrote to Jung, at a time when she was preparing a thesis on the psychology of religion:

And – without knowing me at all – Jung took the trouble to send me an unpublished version of an article of his on the Trinity. When I made my first visit to him ... I was very apprehensive –

Jung with Mary, daughter of Winston Churchill, at the Allmendingen Castle near Berlin, 1946.
It was Mary Churchill's interest in Jung's work that brought him together with her father after the war.

but no sooner had I entered his presence than I felt completely at ease. And everyone I have known since who met him told me the same story. We talked at different times about parapsychology – synchronicity – the occult – and I would go home in the evening and see him sitting there – the chair, his feet, clothes, hands – and I would know it was not a memory image but communication with reality.... You see, he had an uncanny gift of being able to talk to the person inside me who refused to come out.[12]

As Jung pointed out in letters and statements, it was the development of the internal spiritual self that was the heart of his work.

You are quite right, the main interest of my work is not concerned with the treatment of neurosis but rather with the approach to the numinous. But the fact is that the approach to the numinous is the real therapy and inasmuch as you attain to the numinous experiences you are released from the curse of pathology. Even the very disease takes on a numinous character.[13]

Of all my patients past middle life, that is, past thirty-five, there is not one whose ultimate problem is not one of religious attitude. Indeed, in the end every one suffered from having lost that which living religions of every age have given to their believers, and none is really cured who has not regained his religious attitude, which naturally has nothing to do with creeds or belonging to a church.[14]

The end of the war brought "a flood of letters," numerous visitors, the revival of anti-Semitic accusations, and the foundation of the C.G. Jung Institute in Zürich. Theological works, strongly influenced by Jung's psychology of religion, began to appear in print while

Robert Johnson, 1955.
Robert Johnson, therapist and author, helped to bring Jung's teachings and methods to America.

Mandala by Robert Johnson.
Johnson created this mandala
for fellow student and partner
Helen M. Luke, whose move to
America was signaled intuitively
by Jung. He was advised by Jung
to honor his dreams, create
space for inner work, and have
faith in the protective power of
the unconscious.

he himself carried on an extensive correspondence with Catholic and Protestant theologians, as well as Jewish and Eastern religious philosophers.

Author Robert Johnson was then a twenty-seven-year-old student at the Institute and in the early stages of analysis.

One day … I brought one of the great pivotal archetypal dreams which have periodically punctuated my life…. I asked for an hour with Mrs. Jung who was lecturing at the Institute and who appealed to me as a gentle, introverted, dignified person….

It seems that Mrs. Jung discussed my dream with Dr. Jung that evening for Dr. Jung called the school next day and told me, "Please come out here, I want to talk to you." …

Dr. Jung took me into the garden and proceeded to give me a very long lecture on the meaning of my dream, what it meant to me to have contact in this manner with the deep parts of the collective unconscious, how I should live, what I might expect of my life, what I should not attempt, what I could trust, what did not belong to me in life. The meeting took nearly three hours and it was clear that I was to listen and not interrupt. Non-directive counselling, indeed! Dr. Jung advised me to spend most of my time alone, have a separate room in the house to be used for nothing but inner work, never to join any organization or collectivity. He indicated that though it was true that I was a young man, my dream was of the second half of life and was to be lived no matter what age I was. When such a dream comes it is to be honored whether the time or circumstances are convenient or not. Dr. Jung told me that the unconscious would protect me, give me everything I needed for my life and that my one duty was to do my inner work. All else would follow from this.[15]

Dr. George Hogle was trying to find answers to life while vacationing in Zürich after time spent post-war in Germany. On impulse he contacted Jung's office to be given an appointment at Bollingen.

After a walk through the woods to what looked like a fairy-tale castle by the side of the lake, the great wooden door was opened to my knock by the huge old hired man, smoking a pipe and with an axe in his hand. In lame German I asked for Herr Doctor, and in idiomatic English he introduced himself – not the dignified professor I had expected. As we stood on the beautiful shore he put me somewhat at ease, chatting about his building of his hideaway. My hesitance and inhibitions were replaced soon after by the conviction that here was a very fallible, rigid old man, as we got into an enormously heated argument about the international situation.

Having helped me realize he was quite human and that it was quite safe to show some feeling, he escorted me up to an elegant Swiss tea which we shared with Emma Jung. They enquired at length about the situation in Germany, no doubt the reason he was willing to see a non-German coming recently out of that country. I knew nothing of the controversy regarding his questionable sympathies for the Germans, but certainly at that time I got no impression that he had ever been warm in any way toward Nazism, rather that he only tried to understand what it all meant at a deeper level.

Finally we were alone for about an hour, during which he dealt graciously and helpfully with my impossible enquiry as to what I should do with my life, knowing nothing about me, and yet no doubt knowing much just by observing. Instead of answering my questions he gave me other, better questions to ask myself over the succeeding months. Most of all as I later mused over the experience of being with this extraordinary man, I felt there must be great worth and depth in an association with

Jung at Küsnacht.

his work. Eleven years later I ... completed my analytic training in London.[16]

Jung, in his seventies, was beginning to feel the toll of the years at many levels.

I ... will soon be seventy-four.... I have to tell myself twice a day: not too much! Snail's pace and rests in between and a change of snail-horses.... I am like an old car with 250,000 km. on its back that still can't shake off the memory of its twenty horsepower. Nevertheless I console myself with the thought that only a fool expects wisdom.[17]

Jung cutting stone at Bollingen, c. 1950.
Jung felt that working with stone helped connect him to his ancestors.

Dear Dr. Oeri....
I know what Albert's death must mean to you, for with him my
last living friend has also departed. We are but a remnant of the
past, more and more so with each coming year. Our eyes turn
away from the future of the human world in which our children,
but not ourselves, will live. Enviable the lot of those who have
crossed the threshold, yet my compassion goes out to those who,
in the darkness of the world, hemmed in by a narrow horizon and

the blindness of ignorance, must follow the river of their days, fulfilling life's task, only to see their whole existence, which once was the present brimming with power and vitality, crumbling bit by bit and crashing into the abyss. This spectacle of old age would be unendurable did we not know that our psyche reaches into a region held captive neither by change in time nor by limitation of place. In that form of being our birth is a death and our death a birth. The scales of the whole hang balanced. With heartfelt sympathy,

Yours sincerely, C.G. Jung[18]

A visit to Bollingen by author and painter Maud Oakes produced this portrait:

Jung was a tall, well-built man – slightly stooped due to his age. His eyes were keen and penetrating with a twinkle in their depth. His mouth was sensitive, humorous, and stubborn, and his whole being gave off a feeling of simplicity, of wisdom and understanding. Jung was a marvelous raconteur and an equally good listener. To me he was a combination of scientist, artist, woodsman, and shaman.[19]

Stone carved by Jung, Bollingen, 1950.
On his seventy-fifth birthday, Jung carved an alchemical inscription as a "thanks offering."

In remembrance of his seventy-fifth birthday Jung chiseled a twenty-inch square stone with three alchemical inscriptions "as a thanks offering." The stone stands outside the tower at Bollingen "and is like an explanation of it."

Here stands the mean, uncomely stone,
'Tis very cheap in price!
The more it is despised by fools,
The more loved by the wise.[20]

When I was working on the stone tablets I became aware of the fateful links between me and my ancestors.... It has always seemed to me that I had to answer questions which fate had posed to my forefathers, and which had not yet been answered, or as if I had to complete, or perhaps continue, things which previous ages had left unfinished.[21]

As there are not only the many but the few, somebody is entrusted with the job of looking ahead and talking of the things to be. That is partially my job, but I have to be careful not to destroy the things that are. Nobody will be so foolish as to destroy the foundations when he is adding an upper story to his house and how can he build it really if the foundations are not yet properly laid.[22]

After the illness a fruitful period of work began for me. A good many of my principal works were written only then. The insight I had had, or the vision of the end of all things, gave me the courage to undertake new formulations. I no longer attempted to put across my own opinion, but surrendered myself to the current of my thoughts. Thus one problem after the other revealed itself to me and took shape.[23]

ANSWER TO JOB

The problem of evil had occupied Jung since his childhood, raising, as it does, fundamental questions about the ideas of God we live with in the form of images, concepts, and metaphors and their consequent effect on the meaning and conduct of human existence. Patients and public had put these questions to him for years. In *Aion* he began tackling the issue of "the dark side of God" but found it needed a more direct focus.

The fateful *Answer to Job* was foreshadowed by a long dream ending in a scene which demonstrated underlying attitudes of the dreamer:

It was a high, circular room with a gallery running along the wall, from which four bridges led to a basin-shaped center. The basin rested upon a huge column and formed the sultan's round seat.... The whole was a gigantic mandala....

I suddenly saw that from the center a steep flight of stairs ascended to a spot high up on the wall.... At the top of the stairs was a small door, and my father said, "Now I will lead you into the highest presence." Then he knelt down and touched his forehead

to the floor. I imitated him, likewise kneeling, with great emotion. For some reason I could not bring my forehead quite down to the floor – there was perhaps a millimeter to spare....

I ... ought really to have touched my forehead to the floor, so that my submission would be complete. But

Demon of the Plague; from *Feldbuch der Wundarzney*, Strasbourg, 1540.
The question of evil in a God-directed universe has plagued man's understanding for millennia. The problem of undeserved suffering is addressed in the biblical story of Job, the favored of God.

Anthony: "What Is the Object of all this?" / The Devil: "There is no Object."; plate XVIII from *Tentation de Saint-Antoine*, the third series, 1896. Lithograph by Odilon Redon.

Satan, an angel of God, was used by Him to test Job.

something prevented me from doing so entirely, and kept me just a millimeter away. Something in me was saying, "All very well, but not entirely." Something in me was defiant and determined not to be a dumb fish: and if there were not something of the sort in free men, no Book of Job would have been written several hundred years before the birth of Christ. Man always has some mental reservation, even in the face of divine decrees. Otherwise, where would be his freedom? And what would be the use of that freedom if it could not threaten Him who threatens it?[24]

A fitting approach to Job! But it took a stronger prod from within "to overcome the greatest inner resistances" and find the courage to write a book which he knew would unleash a storm against him.

If there is anything like the spirit seizing one by the scruff of the neck, it was the way this book came into being....

It came upon me suddenly and unexpectedly during a feverish illness....

It was as if accompanied by the great music of a Bach or a Handel.... I did not hear anything. I just had the feeling of listening to a great composition.... I felt its contents as an unfolding of the divine consciousness in which I participate like it or not. It was reassuring for my inner balance that I made myself conscious of this development.[25]

The story of Job from the Old Testament, dated 600–300 BCE, confronts us with an ambivalent, contradictory God image. Job, an upright man who leads a blameless life according to the law and his religion, becomes the victim of a bet between God and his son Satan. Would Job stay faithful to God if he lost everything he had – his children, herds, health, the goodwill of his wife and friends – if he were denied a fair trial by a judge, and ended up with death pounding at his door?

Reeling under the fisticuffs of fate dealt by Satan, with God's permission, Job angrily debates his case before God, asking: "Why me?" He seeks God's help against God, thereby recognizing God's divided nature as both "Redeemer" and "Terrible." God thunders. Job gives up asking for justice and surrenders as a created being subject both to death and the omnipotence of the Creator – "I know that my Redeemer lives" – and survives the whole ordeal.

Jung's *Answer to Job* meets current Christian thinking of "*privatio boni*" head on. Christianity sees evil as an absence of good, something extraneous to God for which man is wholly responsible. Jung recognizes "the divine darkness" revealed in the Book of Job and argues good and evil as halves of a paradoxical whole, both of which are contained in the concept of God, an idea long held in Eastern religions.

Psychological experience shows that whatever we call "good"

Christ and the Devil; engraving by Johann Sadler, Paris, 1582.
Jung's *Answer to Job* offended many by recognizing "divine darkness," the paradox of both good and evil being contained in God as One. Jung cited Clement of Rome, who taught that God rules with Christ at his right hand and the Devil at his left.

is balanced by an equally substantial "bad" or "evil." If "evil" is non-existent, then whatever there is must needs be "good." Dogmatically, neither "good" nor "evil" can be derived from Man since the "Evil One" existed before Man as one of the "Sons of God." The idea of the *privatio boni* began to play a role in the Church only after Mani.

Before this heresy, Clement of Rome taught that God rules with a right and a left hand, the right being Christ, the left Satan. Clement's view is clearly monotheistic as it unites the opposites in one God.

Later Christianity, however, is dualistic, inasmuch as it splits off one half of the opposites, personified in Satan, and he is eternal in his state of damnation.... If Christianity claims to be a monotheism, it becomes unavoidable to assume the opposites as being contained in God.[26]

Many theologians were shocked by this. The German edition upset representatives of three religions. Most critics were hostile. Jung speaks of "an avalanche of prejudice, misunderstanding, and atrocious stupidity." American publishers were afraid to print it for a time; when they did, it became an unexpected best-seller, inspiring people who only knew the Bible by hearsay to turn to it with curiosity. The best reactions came from the young; the most enthusiastic letters were sent by simple people.

Jung had written it, he said, "not as a biblical scholar but as a layman" who nevertheless "spoke in the name of the many" who felt the same way. Although he had "no idea of announcing any eternal truth" he did hope "to meet with thoughtfulness in the public." Deep feeling often colors his voice in the book and in the intense correspondence that it produced.

To the Reverend Erastus Evans he wrote,

Allow me to tell you that I am profoundly grateful to you for your most remarkably objective review of my uncouth attempt to disturb the obnoxious somnolence of the guardians. That is the way in which this damnable little book looks to me....

I can assure you I am a moral coward as long as possible. As a good little bourgeois citizen, I am lying low and concealed as deeply as possible, still shocked by the amount of the indiscretions I have committed, swearing to myself that there would be no more of it because I want peace and friendly neighborhood and

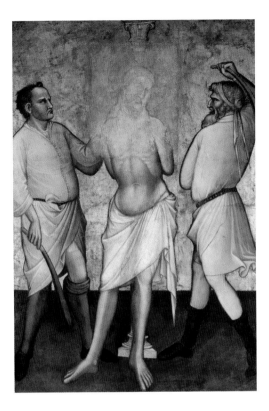

Flagellation of Christ;
tempera by Spinello
Aretino, Florence, *c.* 1400.
Jung called the nature
of God the "mystery of
mysteries." The dual aspect
of God, encompassing
both good and evil, is
correspondingly reflected in
man: "as above, so below."

a good conscience and the sleep of the just. Why should I be the unspeakable fool to jump into the cauldron?

Well, I don't want to be melodramatic. This is just for your personal information. I have no merit and no proper guilt since I got to it "like a dog to a kick," as we say. And the little moral coward I am goes on whining: why should I be always the one that collects all available kicks?

I tell you these things because you have been nice, just, and lenient with me. The attribute "coarse" is mild in comparison to what you feel when God dislocates your hip or when he slays the firstborn....

That is one side of my experiences with what is called "God." "Coarse" is too weak a word for it. "Crude," "violent," "cruel," "bloody," "hellish," "demonic" would be better. That I was not downright blasphemous I owe to my domestication and polite cowardice. And at each step I felt hindered by a beatific vision of which I'd better say nothing.[27]

For years he debated vigorously with Catholic and Protestant theologians alike, over seventy of them, always asserting that he spoke "of the idea or opinion man makes of God to himself," "the God image" and not the nature of God, "the mystery of all mysteries," "Being" beyond thought – always arguing the evolutionary relationship between God and man, man and God.

TO FATHER VICTOR WHITE....

The crux seems to lie in the contamination of the two incongruous notions of Good and of Being. If you assume, as I do, that Good is a moral judgment and not substantial in itself, then Evil is its opposite and just as non-substantial as the first. If however you assume that Good is Being, then Evil can be nothing else than Non-Being....

Things are quite simple if you could only admit that Good and Evil are judgments, having nothing to do with the incommensurable concept of Being....

Is it quite impossible for a theologian to admit the obvious fact of Good and Evil being moral judgments and as such relative to an observer? There is not the faintest evidence for the identity of Good and Being. God is certainly Being itself and you call Him the *Summum Bonum*.[28]

TO THE REV. MORTON T. KELSEY....

It is permissible to assume that the *Summum Bonum* is so good, so high, so perfect, but so remote that it is entirely beyond our grasp. But it is equally permissible to assume that the ultimate reality is a being representing all the qualities of its creation, virtue, reason, intelligence, kindness, consciousness, and their opposites, to our minds a complete paradox. The latter view fits the facts of human existence, whereas the former cannot explain away the obvious existence of evil and suffering. Whence evil? – this age-old question is not answered unless you assume the existence of a supreme being who is in the main unconscious. Such a model would explain why God has created a man gifted with consciousness and why He seeks His goal in him. In this the Old Testament, the New Testament, and Buddhism agree. Meister Eckhart said it: "God is not blessed in his [mere] Godhead. He must be born in man forever." This is what happens in Job: The Creator sees himself through the eyes of man's consciousness and this is the reason why God has to become man, and why man is progressively gifted with the dangerous prerogative of the divine "mind." You have it in Christ's saying: "Ye are gods" and man has not even begun yet to know himself.[29]

In *Answer to Job* Jung sees the duality of the God-image reflected also in humanity: "A paradoxical God image forces man to come to terms with his own paradoxicality." This corresponding conflict of opposites in acute form brings the human being much suffering and trials which, if endured, can be transcended.

Only through the most extreme and menacing conflict does the Christian experience deliverance into divinity, always provided he doesn't break, but accepts the burden of being marked by God. In this way alone can the *imago Dei* realize itself in him and God become man....[30]

The Christian Church has hitherto ... [recognized] Christ as the one and only God-man. But the indwelling of the Holy Ghost, the third Divine Person, in man, brings about a Christification of many, and the question then arises whether these many are all complete God-men.... It is well to remind ourselves of St. Paul and his split consciousness: on one side he felt he was the apostle directly called and enlightened by God, and, on the other side, a sinful man who could not pluck out the "thorn in the flesh" and rid himself of the Satanic angel who plagued him. That is to say even the enlightened person remains what he is, and is never more than his own limited ego before the One who dwells within him, whose form has no knowable boundaries, who encompasses him on all sides, fathomless as the abysms of the earth and vast as the sky.[31]

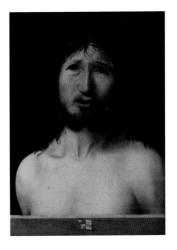

Christ Crowned with Thorns; painting by Antonella da Messina (1430–1479).
Agreeing with Meister Eckhart, Jung said God "must be born in man forever ... the Creator sees himself through the eyes of man's consciousness."

Christ and Buddha; painting by Paul Ranson, *c.* 1890–92.

Jung recognized that all religions reveal God: "I could give none preference over the other."

JUNG AND CHRISTIANITY

Many times Jung used to say to close friends, "They would have burned me as a heretic in the Middle Ages." His relationship to Christianity was that of a critical insider/outsider with a universal point of view.

I positively do not believe that Christianity is the only and the highest manifestation of the truth. There is at least as much truth in Buddhism and in other religions too.[32]

Jesus – Mani – Buddha – Lao-tse are for me the pillars of the temple of the spirit. I could give none preference over the other.[33]

I only wish the theologians would accept the Kabbala and India and China as well so as to proclaim still more clearly how God reveals himself. If in the process Christianity should be relativized up to a point, this would be *ad majorem Dei gloriam* [for the greater glory of God] and would do no harm to Christian doctrine.[34]

For Jung, Christianity was not a static religion founded in a complete state two thousand years ago: "The Christian symbol is a living being that carries the seeds of further development in itself." Although "its foundations remain the same eternally," "Christianity must be interpreted anew in each aeon," otherwise "it suffocates in traditionalism."

We are still looking back to the pentecostal events in a dazed way instead of looking forward to the goal the spirit is leading us to. Therefore mankind is wholly unprepared for the things to come. Man is compelled by divine forces to go forward to increasing consciousness and cognition, developing further and further away from his religious background because he does not understand it any more. His religious leaders and teachers are still hypnotized by the beginning of a then-new aeon of consciousness instead of understanding them and their implications. What was once called the "Holy Ghost" is an impelling force, creating wider consciousness and responsibility and thus enriched cognition. The real history of the world seems to be the progressive incarnation of the deity.[35]

"Progressive incarnation" is not found in blind imitation of the founder of Christianity. Jung asked one theologian, "How do you make it clear to your listeners that Christ's death and resurrection is their death and resurrection?" A metaphoric death and rebirth can be found by taking up our own cross of opposites and living them out as fully and individually as Jesus did his.

Christ ... took himself with exemplary seriousness and lived his life to the bitter end, regardless of human convention and in opposition to his own lawful tradition, as the worst heretic in the eyes of the Jews and a madman in the eyes of his family. But we? We imitate Christ and hope he will deliver us from our own fate. Like little lambs we follow the shepherd, naturally to good pastures. No talk at all of uniting our Above and Below! On the contrary Christ and his cross deliver us from our conflict, which we simply leave alone.... Instead of bearing ourselves, i.e., our own cross, ourselves, we load Christ with our unresolved conflicts. We "place ourselves under his cross," but by golly not under our own.... The cross of Christ was borne by himself and was his. To put oneself under somebody else's cross, which has already been carried by him, is certainly easier than to carry your own cross amid the mockery and contempt of the world. That way you remain nicely ensconced in tradition and are praised as devout. This is well-organized Pharisaism and highly un-Christian. Whoever imitates Christ and has the cheek to want to take Christ's cross on himself when he can't even carry his own has in my view not yet learnt the ABC of the Christian message.

Have your congregation understood that they must close their eyes to the traditional teachings and go through the darkness of their own souls and set aside everything in order to become that which every individual bears in himself as his individual task, and that no one can take this burden from him? We continually pray that "this cup may pass from us" and not harm us. Even Christ did so, but without success.... We might ... discover, among other things, that in every feature Christ's life is a prototype of individuation and hence cannot be imitated: one

Detail of *Christ on the Cross*; bronze, German, *c.* 1000.
Jung saw Christ's death and resurrection as a metaphor for our own death and rebirth.
He suggested that carrying our own cross of opposites as completely as Jesus did his is the
way to true healing.

can only live one's own life totally in the same way with all the consequences this entails.[36]

To Jung, Christianity, as opposed to Christ's teachings, had lost touch with vital elements of life, which it needed to restore to achieve wholeness. "We are cut off from our earth through more than two thousand years of Christian training."[37] This exclusion of nature and animals, the repression of Eros and creative fantasy alienated man from his own instincts as well as from the deeper impersonal forces. In the same way "God-awful legalistic religion" and over-reliance on faith got in the way of *gnosis*, or direct knowing of God. "Religion," he said "is a defense against religious experience."

When Jung was presented with a gift of Volume One of the fourth-century Gnostic documents, discovered at Nag Hammadi in 1945, he found in this "Jung Codex" a confirmation of many of his own ideas, including the individuation process and religion as gnosis.

St. Paul for instance was not converted to Christianity by intellectual or philosophical endeavor or by a belief, but by the force of his immediate experience. His belief was based upon it but our modern theology turns the thing round and holds that we

Ouroboros.

The serpent that eats and recreates itself, the ouroboros is an ancient symbol of eternal becoming, which the Gnostics also used to characterize the cosmos. Jung discovered in fourth-century Gnostic texts (found in 1945) confirmation of many of his own ideas.

first ought to believe, and then we would have an inner experience, but this reversal forces people into a wrong rationalism and excludes even the possibility of a religious experience.[38]

People speak of belief when they have lost knowledge. Belief and disbelief in God are mere surrogates. The naïve primitive doesn't believe in God, he knows, because the inner experience rightly means as much to him as the outer. He still has no theology and hasn't yet let himself be befuddled by booby trap concepts. He adjusts his life – of necessity – to outer and inner facts, which he does not – as we do – feel to be discontinuous. He lives in one world whereas we live only in one half and merely believe in the other or not at all. We have blotted it out with so-called "spiritual development," which means that we live by self-fabricated electric light – and to heighten the comedy – believe or don't believe in the sun.[39]

Jung often weighed the warring opposites within Christianity. While he might plump for Protestant private conscience over Catholic authoritarian collectivism, he deplored the former's loss of ritual and symbolism, its rationalistic, "tied to the Bible," "Christocentric," "one third of the godhead" Christianity. At least Catholicism acknowledged "continuing revelation" and also the feminine principle in Mary as mediatrix and queen of heaven.

He complained, "The fact that I as a Christian struggle to unite Catholicism and Protestantism within myself is chalked up against me in true Pharasaic fashion as blatant proof of lack of character."[40] Yet "finding a mediating position" between the many Christian sects would point to even further development.

Since this world is one world we are faced with the question: How do we come to grips with it? We cannot simply restrict ourselves to our view of the world, but must perforce find a standpoint from which a view will be possible that goes a little step beyond the Christian as well as the Buddhist, etc.... One cannot be simply Protestant or Catholic. That is much too facile, for in the end the one is the other's brother and this cannot be got rid of simply by declaring one of them invalid.[41]

One clergyman Jung tussled with, Pastor Walter Bernet, published extracts of their correspondence in an essay concluding:

Statue of Mary bolted to the ocean floor, coast of South America, 1978; photograph by Rosalie Winard.

Jung, who decried the submergence of the feminine in patriarchal religions, felt it to be partly redeemed by Catholic recognition of Mary as mediatrix and Queen of Heaven.

This outsider of theology has, with the relentless determination with which he demands experience of man, with his uncomfortable criticism of ecclesiastical talk of God, with his bold vision in particular of the Protestant Church, urged upon contemporary theological thought questions which in the interest of theology are absolutely necessary and which in their rigor show the way.[42]

To his friend, Father Victor White, Jung wrote,

No Christian is meant to sleep in a safe pew.... I have discovered in my private life that a true Christian is not bedded upon roses and he is not meant for peace and tranquility of mind but for war. And again I am realizing profoundly that not everybody's nature is as bellicose as mine, although I have attained – *Deo concedente* – a certain state of peace within, paid for by a rather uncomfortable state of war without. But even if a peaceful nature has reached a certain higher level of consciousness he cannot escape the raging conflict of opposites in his soul, as God wants to unite his opposites in man. As soon as a more honest and complete consciousness beyond the collective has been established, man is no more an end in himself, but becomes an instrument of God, and this is really so and no joke about it.[43]

Saint Michael and the Dragon; French engraving, 1644.
Jung wrote that a true Christian is not meant for peace but for war, symbolized here by Saint Michael and the dragon. A conscious human being, by incorporating the opposing forces that battle within, goes on to become "an instrument of God."

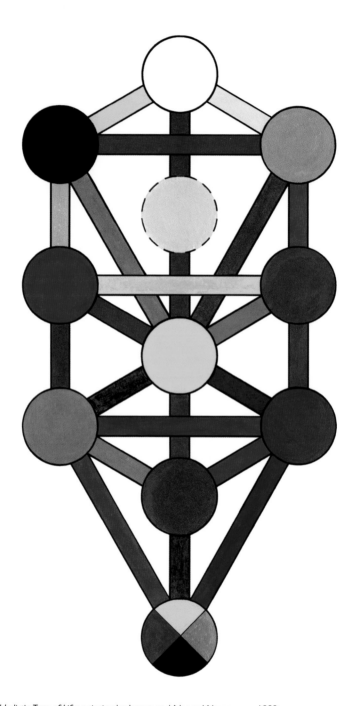

Kabbalistic Tree of Life; painting by James and Nancy Wasserman, 1992.

The "new physics" points to connections seen in esoteric traditions such as Kabbala. Jung saw that his ideas would be vindicated by new discoveries in higher mathematics and science.

SYNCHRONICITY

No sooner had Jung taken on Job, God, and Christian theologians than he added in scientists. His thesis on psychic synchronicity, with its challenge to conventional ideas of time, space, and causality, created a stir in scientific circles. He had often said that his psychology would be accepted and proven, not by his psychiatric colleagues, but by the new physics, and it was an eminent scientist who originally sparked his mind toward synchronicity, a scientist who was himself inspired in his main work by a dream.

> Professor Einstein was my guest on several occasions at dinner.... These were very early days when Einstein was developing his first theory of relativity. He tried to instill into us the elements of it, more or less successfully. As non-mathematicians we psychiatrists had difficulty in following his arguments. Even so, I understood enough to form a powerful impression of him. It was above all the simplicity and directness of his genius as a thinker that impressed me mightily and exerted a lasting influence on my own intellectual work. It was Einstein who first started me off thinking about a relativity of time as well as space, and their psychic conditionality. More than thirty years later this stimulus led to my relation with the physicist Professor W. Pauli and to my thesis of psychic synchronicity.[44]

Jung waited twenty cautious years before publishing his material. When he did, it was in tandem with Wolfgang Pauli, Nobel Prize-winning physicist and friend. In the publication *The Interpretation of Nature and the Psyche*, Pauli contributed an essay on "The Influence of Archetypal Ideas on the Scientific Theories of Kepler." Jung's essay was "Synchronicity: An Acausal Connecting Principle."

For years he had exchanged ideas on the growing relationship between modern physics and psychology with Pauli and other scientists. Both disciplines, he said, "are entering a sphere – the one from without, the other from within – which is unknown. That's the reason for the parleys between psychology and higher mathematics." "In modern physics the possibility that the world has several dimensions is no longer denied."[45]

> Dear Professor Pauli,
> Best thanks for kindly sending me Jordan's paper. I think

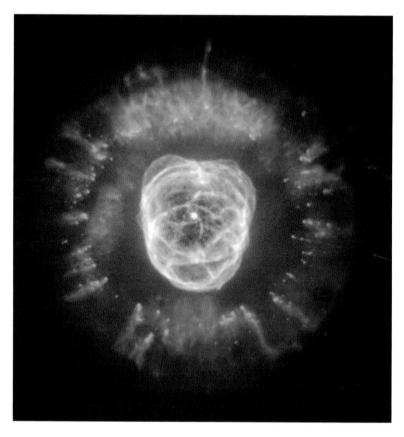

Eskimo Nebula (NGC-2392); photograph by Hubble Space Telescope, NASA, 2000.
Whether seeing our world from the outside or inside, modern physics and modern
psychology both admit the effect of the observer on the observed.

this paper should be published, as it is concerned with the
actual changeover of the physicist's mode of observation to the
psychological field. This paper was inevitable. Having come to
the conclusion that the observed is also a disturbance by the
observer, the consistent investigator of the unknown interior of
the atom could not help seeing that the nature of the observing
process becomes perceptible in the disturbance caused by the
observation. To put it more simply, if you look long enough
into a dark hole you perceive what is looking in. This is also the
principle of cognition in yoga, which derives all cognition from
the absolute emptiness of consciousness.[46]

Dear Professor Jung,
The epistemological situation with regard to the concepts "conscious" and "unconscious" seems to offer a pretty close analogy to the "complementarity" situation in physics. Every "observation of the unconscious," i.e., every conscious realization of unconscious contents, has an uncontrollable reactive effect on these same contents.... It is undeniable that the development of "microphysics" has brought the way in which nature is described in this science very much closer to that of the new psychology.[47]

JUNG TO PROFESSOR NELSON –
The comparison of modern psychology to modern physics is no idle talk. Both disciplines have, for all their diametrical opposition, one most important point in common, namely the fact that they both approach the hitherto "transcendental" region of the Invisible and Intangible, the world of merely analogous thought.[48]

Synchronicity demonstrates the invisible world in action in what Jung called "a creation in time."

Synchronicity states that a certain psychic event is paralleled by some external non-psychic event and that there is no causal connection between them. It is a parallelism of meaning.[49]

As one example of this meaningful coincidence in time, Jung tells of the sudden appearance in the physical world of a beetle resembling a scarab, the Egyptian symbol of rebirth, just as a patient was relating her dream of a golden scarab. A dream foretelling a death or catastrophe that later occurs might be another example. A clock stopping or a glass shattering at the moment of a death would be synchronicity.

Such occurrences have no logical explanation or physical cause. Time and space become relative. Psyche and matter have merged, inner and outer life coincided; not in cause and effect but "a falling together in time – simultaneity."

The point of a synchronous event is its meaningfulness to the experiencer, which in turn signals the larger forces of life operating in the background, the "organizer" of the phenomenon, the transcendental cause. In the Middle Ages this was accepted under the term "correspondences." Chinese science, including the

The Worship of the Scarab; engraving after an Egyptian painting.
Synchronicity operates in "meaningful coincidence," as when Jung observed a beetle at the window just as a patient was describing her dream of a golden scarab, symbol of renewal.

"readable archetypes" of *I Ching*, is based on the same principle.

Jung called synchronicity "acausal orderedness," a principle not contradicting the scientific time, space, and causality modes of Western thinking, but rather a complementary addition to it. Where scientific experimental research is based on regular events that can be repeated and quantified by statistics, synchronicity points to the exception that is hard to verify objectively, though it is subjectively meaningful. Yet "exceptions are facts and cannot be treated as non-existent." They are a "special class of natural events."

> The statistical method of science stands in a relationship of complementarity to synchronicity. This means that when we observe statistically we eliminate the synchronicity phenomena and ... when we establish synchronicity we must abandon the statistical method.[50]

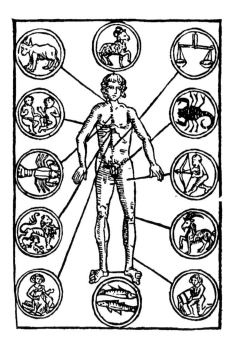

Astrological Correspondences;
woodcut, 1630.

Correspondences are visible in
the lexicon of astrology. Modes of
perception, symbolically organized
as zodiacal "signs," influence areas of
the human body, uniting the cosmos
with man.

The causalism that underlies our scientific picture of the world
breaks everything down into individual processes which it
punctiliously tries to isolate from all other parallel processes.
This tendency is absolutely necessary if we are to gain a
reliable knowledge of the world, but philosophically it has
the disadvantage of breaking up, or obscuring, the universal
interrelationship of events so that a recognition of the greater
relationship, i.e. the unity of the world, becomes more and more
difficult. Everything that happens, however, happens in the same
"one world" and is part of it. For this reason events must have
an a priori aspect of unity.[51]

Modern physics already points in this direction. The traditional scientific concept
of natural law backed by causality has been challenged internally, particularly in the
cosmic arena (the very large) and the subatomic (the very small), where four-
dimensional thinking is now accepted.

Modern physics shattered the absolute validity of natural law
and made it relative ... But if cause and effect turns out to be only
statistically valid and relatively true we have to look for other
factors of explanation in explaining natural processes.[52]

Left-Handed Tantra Yantra #3; painting by Morris Graves, 1982. The "new physics" reminds us that all is energetically connected in physical fact and in psychic meaning.

"Certain phenomena of synchronicity seem to be bound up with the archetypes." Synchronistic events nearly always occur during, or because of, heightened emotion. It's as if the threshold of consciousness is lowered, which then allows the unconscious and its contents to show themselves in conscious life.

These spheres of heightened emotion occur within archetypal situations such as death, mortal danger, catastrophes, mental or physical illness, or relationship crises, which demonstrate innate "patterns of behavior that are universal in character, arousing the same feelings in everyone." Similarly, close-bonded archetypal relationships such as those between mother and child or between lovers often produce synchronistic telepathic communication.

For Jung, the archetypes are "an imprint which presupposes an imprinter";

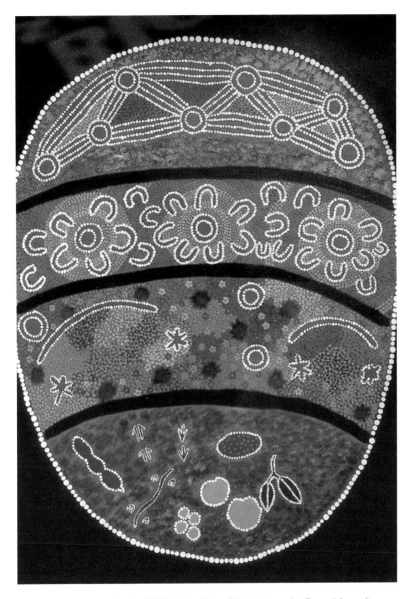

The Four Brains; painting by Rachel Napaljarri Jurra, Waadpiri people, Central Australia, 1992.

Aboriginal philosophy posits four brains for the human experience, four levels that describe our relationship to our world: story brain (Tjukurrpa), myths/thought; family brain (Walytju), relationships/emotions; country brain (Ngurra), geography/environment; body brain (Kurunpa), physical/molecular.

Courtly Lovers; manuscript painting by Reza-ye 'Abbasi, Iran, Safavid Dynasty, 1630.
Lovers throughout history and literature have so bonded that they are "one hand, one heart" and can think each other's thoughts.

"the archetype is only the name of Tao, not Tao itself." And "just as the physicist regards the atom as a model I regard archetypal ideas as sketches for the purpose of visualizing the unknown background."

We ... have to expect a factor in the psyche that is not subject to the laws of time and space, as it is on the contrary capable of suppressing them to a certain extent. In other words: this factor is expected to manifest the qualities of time- and spacelessness, i.e., "eternity" and "ubiquity." Psychological experience knows of such a factor; it is what I call the archetype, which is ubiquitous in time and space, of course relatively speaking. It is a structural element of the psyche we find everywhere and at all times; and it is that in which all individual psyches are identical with each other, and where they function as if they were the one undivided Psyche the ancients called *anima mundi* or the *psyche tou kosmou* [cosmic psyche]. This is no metaphysical speculation but an observable fact, and therefore the key to innumerable mythologies, that is to the manifestations of unconscious fantasy.... It may be, from a psychological point of view, a mere similarity and not a unity in essence ... but here parapsychology comes in, with its psi-phenomena that unmistakably show an essential identity of two separate events, as for instance the act of prevision and the objective precognized fact. These experiences show that the factor in question is one and the same inside and outside the psyche.... In our ordinary minds we are in the worlds of time and space and within the individual psyche. In the state of the archetype we are in the collective psyche, in a world-system whose space-time categories are relatively or absolutely abolished.

This is about as far as we can go safely. I see no way beyond, since we are not capable of functioning in a four-dimensional system at will; it only can happen to us. Our intellectual means reach only as far as archetypal experiences, but within that sphere we are not the motors, we are the moved objects. Experiment in the ordinary sense therefore becomes impossible.... There is no regularity between archetype and synchronistic event....

I think you are correct in assuming that synchronicity, though in practice a relatively rare phenomenon, is an all-pervading factor of principle in the universe, i.e., in the *Unus Mundus*, where there is no incommensurability between so-called matter and so-called psyche. Here one gets into deep waters, at least I myself must confess that I am far from having sounded these abysmal depths.

In this connection I always come upon the enigma of the natural number. I have a distinct feeling that Number is a key to the mystery, since it is just as much discovered as it is invented. It is quantity as well as meaning. For the latter I refer to the arithmetical qualities of the fundamental archetype of the self ... and its historically and empirically well-documented variants of the Four....

It seems that I am too old to solve such riddles, but I do hope that a young mind will take up the challenge. It would be worth while.[53]

With graduation diploma in hand, analyst William Alex went to Jung's home in Zürich to say goodbye.

To my surprise he accompanied me ... down the street toward my parked car. Jung continued to walk beside me silently, pipe in mouth, evidently lost in thought, and I, too, said nothing. Suddenly he turned to me and asked "Why don't they understand me?" There was a tone in his voice I had not heard before that was at once plaintive, questioning, and hurt. I instinctively felt I knew what "they" referred to. "They" was the world out there, the world of science, of academic psychology and psychiatry, of organized religions, of prejudices that persist in misunderstanding and misquoting his discoveries and insights into the inner world, the human soul. I sensed in his question some of the loneliness of the explorer, of the quester who dares to look beyond the accepted and the known; who cannot do otherwise.

I answered "Dr. Jung, you know as well as any man alive why they don't understand you. Is it not because you are probably fifty or a hundred years ahead of your time?" He looked at me for a brief while, nodded quietly, extended his hand for a final handshake.[54]

The Naming; painting by Joe Geshick, Ojibway, 1993.

Jung felt misunderstood by his contemporaries; his loneliness was that of the pioneer, he who dreams alone and visits uncharted territory in order to return and tell of his discoveries.

LETTERS

Although Jung saw a stream of distinguished international visitors, more and more he used letters to keep in touch with the world and to communicate his ideas. Altogether, they are an important aid to the interpretation of his work. He held written discussions with parapsychologist J.B. Rhine, a Japanese philosopher, an Indian biologist, theologians of all persuasions, an Irish priest in remote Donegal, and a Western Australian teacher/author.

He corresponded with international writers Hermann Hesse, James Joyce, Erich Neumann, Miguel Serrano, Sir Laurens van der Post, Sir Herbert Read, Upton Sinclair, J.B. Priestley, H.G. Wells, and Count Keyserling.

The great bulk of his correspondence was with people unknown to him, like the American, describing himself as "just a little fellow, fifty-eight years old and employed as a packer," who wanted Jung's view on reincarnation. To Jung it meant that while "the use of psychotherapy is reserved for medical specialists," what might be called "the 'explanation' reaches a lot more people than I would have thought possible."

I always remember a letter I received one morning, from a woman who wanted to see me just once in her life. The letter made a very strong impression on me, I am not quite sure why. I invited her to come and she came. She was very poor – poor intellectually too. I don't believe she had ever finished primary school. She kept house for her brother; they ran a little newsstand. I asked her kindly if she really understood my books which she said she had read. And she replied in this extraordinary way "Your books are not books, Herr Professor, they are bread."

Sir Laurens van der Post, author, explorer, and scholar (1906–1996).

For many years a student and champion of Jung's ideas, van der Post wrote of Jung's impact on his life.

And the little travelling salesman of women's things, who stopped me in the street and looked at me with immense eyes, saying "Are you really the man who writes those books? Are you truly the one who writes about these things no one knows?"[55]

At times letters to Jung reached "avalanche" proportions, causing him to grumble and complain because they tired him out. Occasionally he ran away from them by tying a bundle in string and hiding them quickly to pretend they hadn't come. But he needed them. They were a balance to an introverted life, and a way of airing his creative thoughts as his energy for scientific work lessened. Jung in his late seventies no longer taught at the C.G. Jung Institute, though Emma did. But twice yearly he invited diploma candidates, like Peter Lynn, to his Küsnacht house for "fireside chats."

He would stand by the fireplace, pipe in mouth, and ask for questions on anything and everything, encouraging us to engage him in dialogue. My most vivid recollection of these extraordinary evenings is the experience of Jung as a giant whose head touched the clouds and whose feet were rooted in the very center of the earth. Within the same sentence he would connect an earthy, peasant-type joke (laughing uproariously) with an obscure pre-Christian myth, both directly relevant to the question under discussion. I used to come away from these gatherings with a great sense of awe, having glimpsed ultimate issues in a thoroughly human context.[56]

James Aylward was Catholic priest as well as Institute student when he met with Jung in his garden.

Jung brings up God as the most proper subject of conversation between two human beings. He says that most people don't look on God as worthy of entry into a salon. People – even theologians – are embarrassed to talk about God. It is more polite to talk about sex.[57]

As Jung was to write later:

The decisive question for man is: Is he related to something infinite or not? That is the telling question of his life. Only if

Man at the Center of the Universe; manuscript painting by Hildegarde of Bingen, from *Codex Latinum, c.* 1200.

For Jung, the burning question for every human being was "Am I related to something infinite or not?" A sense of the infinite helps to ground our lives in essential values.

we know that the thing which truly matters is the infinite can we avoid fixing our interests upon futilities, and upon all kinds of goals which are not of real importance.... If we understand and feel that here in this life we already have a link with the infinite, desires and attitudes change. In the final analysis, we count for something only because of the essential we embody, and if we do not embody that, life is wasted. In our relationships to other men, too, the crucial question is whether an element of boundlessness is expressed in the relationship.

The feeling for the infinite, however, can be attained only if we are bounded to the utmost.... Only consciousness of our narrow confinement in the self forms the link to the limitlessness of the unconscious. In such awareness we experience ourselves concurrently as limited and eternal, as both the one and the other.[58]

TONI

In March 1953, while Jung was still writing his last big scientific work, Toni Wolff died suddenly in her sleep. She was sixty-five.

> On the day of her death even before I had received the news I suffered a relapse and had a bad attack of my tachycardia. This has now subsided but it has left an arrhythmia which hampers my physical capacities very much.... Toni Wolff's death was so sudden, so totally unexpected that one could hardly realize her passing. I had seen her only two days before. Both of us completely unsuspecting.[59]

Jung and Toni had not seen as much of each other as usual in her last years. Her

The Divine Land; gouache by Cecil Collins, 1979.
Jung spoke to a friend of a magical island where lived the "mystic flower of the soul," alluding to Toni Wolff.

Toni Wolff in the garden at Bollingen.
Jung sought to get Toni Wolff's scientific work published after her death in 1953.

retirement as president of the Psychological Club in 1948 after twenty distinguished years had taken her out of the limelight, while a severe arthritic condition had made the Bollingen retreat too primitive for her health to sustain, though she continued her analytic work to the end. And, regardless of outer circumstance, Jung's attention toward her may have diminished.

It has been said of Toni Wolff that "of all those closest to Jung she suffered most." To friend and colleague Barbara Hannah, Toni said once that on no account did she want to outlive Jung. He in turn confided that, as Toni was thirteen years younger than he, "I never seriously considered the possibility that she could die before me." His own health prevented him from going to the funeral, although Emma attended the memorial service.

In a letter to a friend, Jung wrote,

The loss of Fräulein Wolff has hit me very hard indeed. She has left behind in her circle a gap that can never be filled.[60]

Barbara Hannah describes Jung's reaction:

Outwardly he kept extremely calm, so that both his wife and his secretary told me they thought he had overcome the shock after a few days, but from my notes for April 1953, I see that he said himself that his pulse was still between eighty and 120; moreover this trouble continued for some time. He had been helped, it is true, by seeing Toni in a dream ... on Easter Eve, looking much taller and younger than she had been when she died, and exceedingly beautiful. She was wearing a frock of all the colors of a bird of paradise, with the wonderful blue of the kingfisher as the most emphasized color. He saw just her image, there was no action in the dream, and he was especially impressed by having dreamed it on the night of the resurrection.[61]

In 1958, Jung initiated efforts to have Toni Wolff's writings published.

Dear Dr. Brody....
I feel the need to recommend the collected papers of Toni Wolff to your attention.... They are distinguished not only by their intellectual content but by the fact that the author had personally experienced the development of analytical psychology from the fateful year of 1912 right up to the recent past and was thus

in a position to record her reactions and sympathetic interest from the first. Her papers also have a documentary value. Even those who did not know the author personally will glean from them an impression of the versatility and depth of her spiritual personality.[62]

When Toni's *Studies in Jungian Psychology* was published, Jung wrote in the introduction that he was "discharging a debt of thanks [to] my friend and collaborator for more than forty years" who "took an active part in all phases of the development of analytical psychology" including "working out practical methods of analysis and ... the task of theoretical formulation" plus "a silent experiment in group psychology ... which constitutes the life of the Psychological Club in Zürich." He pointed to "her high natural intelligence and quite exceptional psychological insight," saying "these essays are uncommonly instructive and stimulating."

The privacy of their personal relationship he preserved by destroying Toni's letters to him and his to her. Six years later, in discussing the story of the Queen of Sheba with its chronicler Miguel Serrano, Jung spoke "of a magic kind of love never for matrimony" and of mystic weddings that were "in reality a process of mutual individuation."

Jung went on as if talking to himself, "Somewhere there was once a Flower, a Stone, a Crystal, a Queen, a King, a Palace, a Lover and his Beloved, and this was long ago, on an Island somewhere in the ocean five thousand years ago.... Such is Love, the Mystic Flower of the Soul. This is the Center, the Self...."

Jung spoke as if in a trance.

"Nobody understands what I mean" he said, "only a poet could begin to understand." ...

"You are a poet," I said, moved by what I had heard. "And that woman, is she still alive?" I asked.

"She died eight years ago.... I am very old."[63]

Anastasis I; painting by Alex Rapoport, 1996.
Jung wrote of the need for "conscious suffering." We can "wake up" to a fuller existence only when we are willing to bear our own burden in life.

Jung in his garden at age eighty, 1955.

Even in old age, Jung exuded a palpable authority and power sensed by those who consulted him.

FOUR DECADES ON

Approaching the age of seventy-nine, a tiring Jung, with all his experience and erudition, still encountered old recurring patterns of depression and doubt about himself, "appalled by the inadequacy of what I have done." It was one polarity of his range of being, though now the personal could be enlarged into an understanding of life's inevitable flow, shaded dark as well as light.

I observe myself in the stillness of Bollingen, with the experience of almost eight decades now, and I have to admit that I have found no plain answer to myself. I am in doubt about myself as much as ever, the more so the more I try to say something definite. It is even as though through familiarity with oneself one became still more alienated![64]

In a letter to his friend Father Victor White, he wrote of the necessity of conscious suffering.

There is no place where those striving after consciousness could find absolute safety. Doubt and insecurity are indispensable components of a complete life. Only those who can lose this life really can gain it. A "complete" life does not consist in a theoretical completeness, but in the fact that one accepts, without reservation, the particular fatal tissue in which one finds oneself embedded, and that one tries to make sense of it or to create a cosmos from the chaotic mess into which one is born. If one lives properly and completely, time and again one will be confronted with a situation of which one will say: "This is too much. I cannot bear it any more." Then the question must be answered: "Can one really not bear it?"[65]

Man has to cope with the problem of suffering. The Oriental wants to get rid of suffering by casting it off. Western man tries to suppress suffering with drugs. But suffering has to be overcome, and the only way to overcome it is to endure it.[66]

Aniela Jaffé characterized Jung, aged eighty:

In 1955 his tall figure was slightly bent and even gave an impression of fragility. Yet most people overlooked this, because it paled beside the massive strength, the powerfulness that radiated from him; no one who ever met him could escape its aura. It was not the powerfulness of an authoritarian; Jung was too good-natured for that, too kindly, too outgoing even in old age and his humor too infectious. Nor was it the powerfulness one associates with erudition or with a highly differentiated and richly endowed intellect.... What was so palpably impressive about him sprang from the superiority of a man who had engaged in a life-and-death struggle with the creative daemon and mastered him, but on whom the struggle had left its mark. This kind of powerfulness is profoundly human, does not arouse fear, is not crushing, does not embarrass or make you feel small, but changes you; it compels veneration and awe.[67]

It was a big year for Jung, with an honorary doctorate of science from the Swiss Technological Institute and two publications – Volume One of *Mysterium Coniunctionis*, compiled in collaboration with Marie-Louise von Franz, and the psychological commentary on *The Tibetan Book of the Great Liberation*. The old anti-Semitic accusations surfaced again, this time to a powerful public rebuttal by a group of Jewish followers.

His eightieth birthday was celebrated at home, followed by several public receptions in Zürich, echoing those in Jungian strongholds in London, New York, San Francisco, and Calcutta. Publicly he could be seen to enjoy the informal Institute party best, for all the newness of most of its teeming guests to him.

Those are the people who will carry on my psychology – people who read my books and let me silently change their lives. It will not be carried on by the people on top, for they mostly give up Jungian psychology and take to prestige psychology instead.[68]

Jung found, to his amusement, that he was becoming a tourist attraction "like the Berne bears" with boats steering past his home, sometimes blowing horns and ringing bells to his answering wave.

Writers and journalists wanted interviews for print, radio, and television – Alberto Moravia, Mircea Eliade, Stephen Black, and John Freeman for the BBC, Charles Baudouin and others for French, English, Swiss, and American publications, including *Time*.

Tibetan demon binding charm and incantation containing *Om-mani-padme-hum*, woodcut, Nepal.
In 1955 Jung published a commentary on *The Tibetan Book of the Great Liberation*, based on his reading of the Eastern manual for progressing through different states of consciousness.

In one interview, Jung cited intellectual kinships with Goethe and Faust, with William James, whom he'd met several times, and with the eighteenth-century Hasidic Rabbi Ber. In another, Stephen Black likened Jung to a typical Swiss peasant, to which he smilingly replied, "That is what I have often been called."

As he wrote to Mary Bancroft in America,

I have appeared in the world, if that is good for me. My name enjoys an existence quasi-independent of myself. My real self is actually chopping wood in Bollingen and cooking the meals, trying to forget the trial of an eightieth birthday.[69]

Carl and Emma Jung at tea in their garden, Küsnacht, 1955.

That didn't keep him from deep conversations in Zürich, as poet, author, and psychotherapist Sheila Moon recalled.

In each of my hours with Dr. Jung I was aware of his sense of urgency about man's religious task, of his intense concern that each of us must be related to ourselves and to God not only inwardly but in the world, if we and the world are not to be destroyed. "We fear our serpent," he said, "as we also fear the *numinosum* – so we run from it.... All we have to give the world and God is ourselves as we are. But this is the hardest of all tasks. Most of us want others to do it for us, to carry us along." ... Over and again he stressed his belief that "unless we live these things we profess, we are useless."

My last sight of him was in 1955 in Ascona. I had photographed him with Mrs. Jung, seated at a table in the warm sunlight outside their hotel by the lake. Very Swiss, very solid, very genuine, very warm, they sat side by side, smiling, as we drove away.[70]

EMMA

I found Mrs. Jung the most integrated person in Zürich....

I found myself deeply moved by a woman who had so obviously found herself and her own authenticity in the midst of so many collective pressures. She was the wife of Carl Jung, which was certainly not an easy task. And she maintained – or rather, achieved – an individuality separate from his. She became a scholar in later years which culminated in her excellent book, *The Legend of the Holy Grail*. Also she became a wise and sensitive analyst, pointing simply and directly to what needed to be looked at. She was a joy to work with....

Mrs. Jung's quiet, penetrating, active and participating attitude helped one always to know that one was working in a religious process where the unconscious was revealing – in even the slightest way – powers greater than the ego. But always I remember how she stressed the role of the ego in the development of consciousness.

Mrs. Jung said to me, "There are egos and egos and egos. The problem is to find the right one." To me, as I saw her, she had found hers and had related it to the deeper archetypal powers making for wholeness.[71]

Emma Jung, 1955.
Wife, teacher, analyst, writer, mother of five, grandmother; Emma's dignity and equanimity is apparent in this portrait in the year of her death.

On May 6, Jung wrote to Victor White:

Dear Victor,
The serious illness of my wife has consumed all my spare time. She has undergone an operation so far successfully, but it has left her in a feeble state needing careful nursing for several weeks to come.[72]

In November, Australian author and teacher Rix Weaver had a meeting with Jung in his study in Küsnacht.

Jung was called away ... and I waited quite awhile. When he returned there was a change. He told me the doctor had just called and that his dear wife wouldn't recover. I offered to leave but he bade me stay. He then sat a little longer to speak. This time he said that life has to be lived fully. One has to live what one is, utilize one's potential. He spoke of his wife's life and its completeness, then added, "Death is a drawing together of two worlds, not an end. We are the bridge."[73]

Five days later, on November 27, 1955, Emma Jung died.

Dear Neumann,
Deepest thanks for your heartfelt letters.... I am sorry that I can only set down these dry words, but the shock I have experienced is so great that I can neither concentrate nor recover my power of speech. I would have liked to tell the heart that you have opened to me in friendship that two days before the death of my wife I had what one can only call a great illumination which, like a flash of lightning, lit up a centuries-old secret that was embodied in her and had exerted an unfathomable influence on my life. I can only suppose that the illumination came from my wife, who was then mostly in a coma, and that the tremendous lighting up and release of insight had a retroactive effect upon her, and was one reason why she could die such a painless and royal death.
    The quick and painless end – only five days between the final diagnosis and death – and this experience have been a great comfort to me. But the stillness and the audible silence about me, the empty air and the infinite distance are hard to bear.[74]

At the funeral, in a packed church in Küsnacht, Jung led in his family of five children and nineteen grandchildren.

Afterwards friends found him alone in his study, sobbing repeatedly, "She was a queen. She was a queen."[75]

After the death of my wife ... I saw her in a dream which was like a vision. She stood at some distance from me, looking at me squarely. She was in her prime, perhaps about thirty, and wearing the dress which had been made for her many years before by my cousin the medium. It was perhaps the most beautiful thing she had ever worn. Her expression was neither joyful nor sad, but, rather, objectively wise and understanding, without the slightest emotional reaction, as though she were beyond the mist of affects. I knew that it was not she, but a portrait she had made or commissioned for me. It contained the beginning of our relationship, the events of fifty-three years of marriage, and the end of her life also. Face to face with such wholeness one remains speechless, for it can scarcely be comprehended.[76]

Jung at Bollingen, c. 1950s.
In times of stress, Jung found that carving in stone gave him "inner stability."

I Ching diagram.
In his foreword to R. Wilheim's translation of the *I Ching*, Jung wrote of the Chinese symbols as "readable" archetypes.

Following a visit to his daughter Marianne, Jung wrote,

Dear Marianne,
Warmest thanks for your lovely letter which was a great joy. I am glad you weren't bored with me. It was a joy to be together with you for a while....

Mama's death has left a gap for me that cannot be filled. So it is good if you have something you want to carry out and can turn to when the emptiness spreads about you too menacingly. The stone I am working on gives me inner stability with its hardness and permanence and its meaning governs my thoughts.[77]

Laurens van der Post recorded a late conversation he had with Jung:

He told me toward the end of his life ... [he] was carving in stone ... some sort of memorial of what Emma Jung and Toni Wolff had brought to his life. On the stone for his wife he was cutting the Chinese symbols meaning "She was the foundation of my house." On the stone intended for Toni Wolff he wanted to inscribe another Chinese character to the effect that she was the fragrance of the house.[78]

MYSTERIUM
CONIUNCTIONIS

The publication of Jung's deepest book, *Mysterium Coniunctionis*, was met with "stony incomprehension ... at least for the time being." Although he wrote, "I have resigned myself to being posthumous," he also confessed, "sometimes I feel like an anachronism even to myself."[79]

The King Greets the Queen; from Salomon Trismosin, *Splendor Solis*, 1582.
Mystical marriage, the *coniunctio* or chemical combination through "affinity," is a form of mystic sexuality symbolizing spiritual union with our source.

Lingam and Yoni Draped with Pearls; painting on wood, back cover of a Saiva manuscript, Nepal, *c.* 1450.

Indian symbolism associates cosmic unification and transformation with the combination of the lingam and the yoni. The union is the font of creativity from which new life flows.

Loneliness does not come from having no people about one, but from being unable to communicate the things that seem important to oneself, or from holding certain views which others find inadmissible.[80]

Like all his late works, *Mysterium Coniunctionis* had been incubating for decades. It represented a deeper turn of the spiral begun with *The Psychology of the Transference* and *Psychology and Alchemy*. It had its genesis in his own life – in his original grasp of the mystical aspect of sexuality, reportedly met within the role of guiding spirit or *soror mystica* experienced with Toni Wolff,[81] and again in the mystical wedding encountered during his near-death experience, both symbolized in the work of medieval alchemy.

The fact that the very idea of mystical marriage was to play such an important role in alchemy is not surprising, inasmuch as the expression usually used for it, *coniunctio*, refers primarily to what is today called chemical combination, and what brings together the elements to be combined is today known as "affinity;" but earlier various designations were used which all expressed human, and in particular, erotic relationships, such as *nuptiae* (wedding), *matrimonium* and *coniugium* (marriage), *amicitia* (friendship), *attractio* (attraction) and *adulatio* (flirtation).[82]

In *Mysterium Coniunctionis*, Jung synthesizes aspects common to alchemy, Gnosticism, Christian mythology, and Indian Tantrism through the symbol of the *hierosgamos* or mystic wedding. He saw, too, that the sixteenth-century alchemistic stages of first separating and then uniting the opposites parallels the individuation process. The symbols that emerge are very much the same as those produced in contemporary dreams or meditation.

Similarly, what raises the individual to a higher level of consciousness is the combining of what has first been separated. The outward combining process, be it sex, chemistry, or religious act, is symbolic of an inward state of unification and transformation. Ultimately the whole human being merges with the Ground of All Being, echoing universal mystic experience.

For the alchemists, the first and second stages result in the oneness of mind and soul with the body.

The third and highest degree of conjunction was the union of the whole man with the *unus mundus* ... the potential world of the first day of creation, when nothing was yet "*in actu*," i.e. divided into two and many but was still one ... the eternal Ground of all empirical being....

The third degree of conjunction is universal: it is relation or identity of the personal with the suprapersonal *atman*, and of the individual tao with the universal tao....

He [the alchemist Dorn] expressly meant not a fusion of the individual with his environment, or even his adaptation to it, but a *unio mystica* with the potential world.... Undoubtedly the idea of the *unus mundus* is founded on the assumption that the multiplicity of the empirical world rests on an underlying unity

Chakrasamvara and Vajravarahi in Union; painting on cotton, Nepal, *c.* 1450.
The union of Tantric deities can embody *unio mystica* at the levels of the synthesis of opposites: the conscious and unconscious, the personal and suprapersonal.

... everything different and divided belongs to one and the same world....

All that is not encompassed by our knowledge, so that we are not in a position to make any statements about its total nature.... But this much we do know beyond all doubt, that empirical reality has a transcendental background.... The common background of microphysics and depth psychology is as much physical as psychic and therefore neither, but rather a third thing, a neutral nature which can at most be grasped in hints since in essence it is transcendental.... The transcendental psychophysical background corresponds to a "potential world." ...

The third and highest conjunction ... would consist, psychologically, in a synthesis of the conscious with the unconscious. The result of this conjunction or equation is theoretically inconceivable, since a known quantity is combined with an unknown one; but in practice as many far-reaching changes of consciousness result from it as atomic physics has produced in classical physics....

Not unnaturally, we are at a loss to see how a psychic experience of this kind – for such it evidently was – can be formulated as a rational concept. Undoubtedly it was meant as the essence of perfection and universality, and, as such, it characterized an experience of similar proportions. We could compare this only with the ineffable mystery of the *unio mystica*, or tao, or the content of *samadhi*, or the experience of *satori* in Zen, which would bring us to the realm of the ineffable and of extreme subjectivity where all the criteria of reason fail. Remarkably enough this experience is an empirical one in so far as there are unanimous testimonies from the East and West alike, both from the present and from the distant past, which confirm its unsurpassable subjective significance.... It is and remains a secret of the world of psychic experience and can be understood only as a numinous event.[83]

Lion at Rest; manuscript painting, India, Mughal period, *c.* 1585.

Even at rest there is an alert readiness in the bearing of a lion, who is a prime symbol of royal power and astrologically of solar power. Jung was born under the zodiac sign of Leo.

LATE COMPANY

While the widowed Jung had daughters and a daughter-in-law to stay with him in turns, he was looked after on a day-to-day basis by two women. Ruth Bailey, an old friend of the family, was invited to "come and see me out" as companion-housekeeper. "You're an old humbug," she would say to him when he seemed to contradict himself and he would roar with laughter and answer, "You're quite right."[84]

Aniela Jaffé, ex-patient, friend, and administrative secretary of the Jung Institute was called in as private secretary. To both women he gave the same warning:

I was expected, Jung explained, never under any circumstances to allow myself to be irritated by his anger, nor his occasional "grumbling," his roaring and cursings...!

In the early days of my secretaryship I was often on tenterhooks as Jung read through the letters I put before him for signature. Every typing mistake was reproachfully and copiously commented on, but what a recompense it was when in his zeal he went too far and found himself in error! I soon learnt to turn the tables on him and use the weapon that never failed: I made him laugh or at least tried to. When a tempest had really broken loose, however, this weapon no longer worked, and then there was no recourse but to ask oneself, in all seriousness, how one had precipitated the storm, and stand up to it. In spite of his preliminary warning, it was anything but easy to let his rage pass over my head. But if I succeeded and managed to appear for work the next day unshaken and unhurt, nobody was more grateful than he. Although most times no further mention was made of the tempest, now and then ... a word was dropped or something unexpected happened, that expressed his thanks. The preciousness of these responses caused the importance of the bygone to shrink to nothing.... The rare occasions when "gale force ten" was reached, Jung out of genuine magnanimity begged my pardon.

His impatience was due not only to his temperament – astrologically he was a Leo – but also to his extreme sensitivity, which both enriched and burdened his life. It was an enrichment because it gave him ... extraordinarily differentiated awareness

Detail of an Attic vase, *c.* 490 BCE. Hermes, the Great Riddler with boots as swift as thought, became the Roman Mercury, who gave his intelligence to the later alchemists in their quest to transmute lead into gold.

... it was a burden because it encroached upon the personal realm and manifested itself as touchiness. Jung was touchy, his feelings were easily hurt and needed sparing in order to display themselves....

He began telling me about himself and the sensitiveness that had tormented him from early youth, how it had encumbered him in his relationships and made him feel unsure of himself, how ashamed it had made him feel, but how, because of this same impressionability, he had perceived beauties and experienced things other people scarcely dreamed of.[85]

Jaffé confessed that the "10 a.m. approach of the old magician never lost its excitement." An "immense" correspondence, writing, which was always toil for him, and visitors took up the working day. For relaxation, Jung played solitaire in the evenings, occasionally "helping fate a little by switching the cards around" in "unabashed cheating." Detective stories, especially Simenon, and English thrillers "lay around everywhere," the detective considered "a modern version of the alchemical Mercurius, solver of all riddles." Science fiction ranked up with them in popularity.

Music he listened to sparingly because, as he told pianist Margaret Tilly, "music is dealing with such deep archetypal material and those who play don't realize this. Yet, used therapeutically from this level, music should be an essential part of every analysis."[86] It "expresses in sounds what fantasies and visions express in visual images ... music represents the movement, development and transformation of motifs of the collective unconscious."[87]

Jaffé reports "a penchant for Negro spirituals" along with Bach, Handel, Mozart, and early music. A string quartet of Schubert had to be turned off because "it moved him too much," while Beethoven's late quartets "churned him up almost beyond endurance." "Bach," he said to a friend, "speaks to God. I am gripped by Bach. But I could slay a man who plays Bach in banal surroundings."[88]

Bollingen continued to be his place of renewal where he customarily played his childlike games, which served as release whenever he got stuck in a problem.

As the neighboring Henry K. Fierz observed,

One could often meet Jung, sitting before his tower, pondering about I do not know what, and playing with a little watercourse, using a little garden shovel fixed to a broomstick. The also very old man, Mr. Kuhn, who looked after the tower … once said to me, "If one sees the Professor, sitting and playing like this, if one would not know that this is a world-famous scientist, one would think that this is a very queer man who behaves in a rather odd way."[89]

It was only now that Bollingen reached completion – materially and symbolically.

Sound, Point; painting by Francesco Clemente, 1990.
In later life, Jung believed music should be an essential part of active therapy and said it expressed in sound the collective unconscious.

After my wife's death ... I felt an inner obligation to become what I myself am. To put it in the language of the Bollingen house, I suddenly realized that the small central section which crouched so low, so hidden was myself! I could no longer hide myself behind the "maternal" and the "spiritual" towers. So, in that same year, I added an upper story to this section, which represents myself, or my ego-personality. Earlier, I would not have been able to do this; I would have regarded it as presumptuous self-emphasis. Now it signified an extension of consciousness achieved in old age. With that the building was complete.[90]

Dear Aniela....
I have finished painting the ceiling in Bollingen and done more work on my inscription and – last but not least – rebricked the rivulets to prevent seepage and cooked some good meals and found and bought an excellent wine. All this has rested me and cured me of various vexations. But I won't speak of that. Thank heavens I have no idea how great is the disorder or order of my correspondence. My memory has the most astonishing holes in it, so that I often catch myself forgetting not only what I have done but more especially what I have not done.[91]

At eighty-two, silence and solitude were prime needs. Noise he fled "whenever

and wherever possible" because it not only disturbed the concentration needed for his work but also "forces me to make the additional psychic effort of shutting it out." Modern noise like "technological gadgetry," gramophone, radio, and "now the blight of television," he described as something that was "predominantly extroverted and abhors all inwardness. It is an evil with deep

Jung on a wall at Bollingen, c. 1955.
In his eighties, Jung needed solitude as a "fount of healing," and silence to overcome the "torment" of talking.

Silence; painting by Odilon Redon, *c.* 1911.
Harpocrates, the god of silence, expresses a soul-gesture demonstrating the need to hold in our energy in order to hear our inner voice.

roots" because "it drowns the inner instinctive warning" and "all goes together with the spiritual disorientation of our time."[92]

> Solitude is for me a fount of healing which makes my life worth living. Talking is often a torment for me, and I need many days of silence to recover from the futility of words. I have got my marching orders and only look back when there's nothing else to do. This journey is a great adventure in itself, but not one that can be talked about at great length. What you think of as a few days of spiritual communion would be unendurable for me with anyone, even my closest friends. The rest is silence! This realization becomes clearer every day as the need to communicate dwindles.[93]

MEMORIES, DREAMS, REFLECTIONS

Jung's main communications with the general public were still to come. His "autobiography" he came to reluctantly; it was "the one thing I'm not going to write" he had said in 1948. Strictly speaking, it is not an autobiography. He always spoke and wrote of it as "Aniela Jaffé's project," with contributions made by him in the form of childhood, travel, and closing chapters. The title *Memories, Dreams, Reflections* describes it very clearly – events of outer life scarce, those of inner life abounding. It includes what Jaffé termed "Jung's religious testament."

> I often asked Jung for specific data on outward happenings, but I asked in vain. Only the spiritual essence of his life's experience remained in his memory, and this alone seemed to him worth the effort of telling.[94]

His sensitivity to the work's possible reception he explained himself.

> I have guarded this material all my life, and have never wanted it exposed to the world; for if it is assailed, I shall be affected even more than in the case of my other books.... I have suffered enough from incomprehension and from the isolation one falls into when one says things that people do not understand.... The "autobiography" is my life, viewed in the light of the knowledge I have gained from my scientific endeavors.... My life has been in a sense the quintessence of what I have written, not the other way around. The way I am and the way I write are a unity. All my ideas and all my endeavors are myself. Thus the "autobiography" is merely the dot on the i.[95]

Artist Mary Crile visited Jung in that period.

> The last time I saw Jung face to face … I found him much aged but there was the same kindly twinkle behind those penetrating eyes of his. When he said, "Pull up your chair, for I am getting deaf and old and stupid," I could not help smiling as I reminded him that he had made exactly the same remark to me, just eleven

years earlier. He replied with a chuckle "Well, it doesn't seem to get any better." ...

When I asked him what he was writing he said, "My biography.... It is purgatory. Frau Jaffé is writing it but I must check it all because no one knows someone else's life. I have done the first twenty years because one can be more objective there." He paused and then added thoughtfully, "I don't know the meaning of life." As he said this I felt that, even for Jung, who more than anyone else in our day saw life steadily and saw it whole, there still remained an unsolved mystery.[96]

Oedipus Considers the Riddle; detail of bronze by Glyn Warren Philpot, 1930.
As Jung aged, the riddle of the meaning of life remained an enigma, an open mystery to be forever pondered.

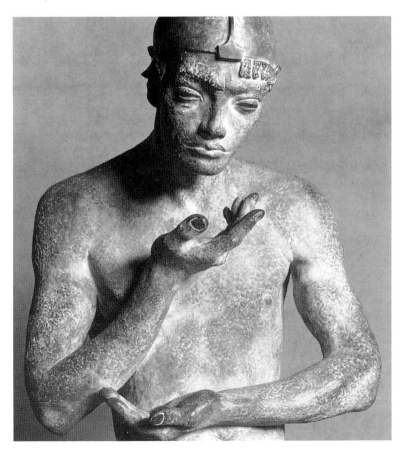

HUMAN BEING

Author Erich Neumann gave this tribute to Jung as a human being:

C.G. Jung is the only really great man I have met in my life, and as a teacher and friend over three decades he has provided me with ever new vital material for love and outrage, with the erratic quality of humanity transcending nature itself. Encountering in a man, with all his weaknesses and in all his greatness, that which is greater than man and in which nonetheless everything human is rooted, was for me a decisive and direction-setting experience.[97]

In the last years of his life, with world events like Soviet suppression of Hungary, the Suez crisis, and Chinese invasion of Tibet as daily dramas, Jung's communication shows repeated concern for the earth, its future, and the individual's role.

The world today hangs by a thin thread, and that is the psyche of man.... It is not the reality of the hydrogen bomb that we need to fear, but what man will do with it.[98]

A change in the attitude of the individual can bring about a renewal in the spirit of the nations.[99]

The whole future, the whole history of the world, ultimately springs as a gigantic summation from these hidden sources in individuals. In our most private and subjective lives we are not only the passive witnesses of our age, and its sufferers, but also its makers. We make our epoch.[100]

We are living in what the Greeks called the right moment for a "metamorphosis of the gods," of the fundamental principles and symbols. This peculiarity of our time, which is certainly not of our conscious choosing, is the expression of the unconscious man within us who is changing....

As at the beginning of the Christian era, so again today we are faced with the problem of the general moral backwardness which has failed to keep pace with our scientific, technical and social progress....

Tibetan Monk at Prayer in Mountain Cell; photograph by Ernst Haas.
Jung was well aware of the ironies of modern life. Here a Tibetan monk has voluntarily walled himself into a mountain cell to pray for the benefit of humankind. Since 1959, the Chinese have outlawed this practice under penalty of imprisonment.

Happiness and contentment, equability of mind and meaningfulness of life – these can be experienced only by the individual and not by a State, which, on the one hand, is nothing but a convention agreed to by independent individuals and, on the other, continually threatens to paralyze and suppress the individual.... The social and political circumstances of the time are certainly of considerable significance, but their importance for the weal or woe of the individual has been boundlessly overestimated in so far as they are taken for the sole deciding

Vision of 1914; painting by C.G. Jung in *The Red Book*, 1920.

Jung, who had visions of destruction before World War I and II, spoke repeatedly of man's power to "destroy his own planet." To offset it, he advocated a more responsible relationship with God.

factors. In this respect all our social goals commit the error of overlooking the psychology of the person for whom they are intended and – very often – of promoting only his illusions.[101]

Everything now depends on man; immense power of destruction is given into his hands, and the question is whether he can resist the will to use it, and can temper his will with the spirit of love and wisdom. He will hardly be able to do so on his own resources. He needs the help of an "advocate" in heaven.[102]

Just as man, as a social being, cannot in the long run exist without a tie to the community, so the individual will never find the real justification for his existence and his own spiritual and moral autonomy anywhere except in an extramundane principle capable of relativizing the overpowering influence of external factors. The individual who is not anchored in God can offer no resistance on his own resources to the physical and moral blandishments of the world. For this he needs the evidence of inner, transcendent experience which alone can protect him from the otherwise inevitable submersion in the mass.[103]

We have become participants of the divine life and we have to assume a new responsibility…. Man's relationship to God probably has to undergo a certain important change: Instead of the propitiating praise to an unpredictable king or the child's prayer to a loving father, the responsible living and fulfilling of the divine love in us will be our form of worship of, and commerce with, God. His goodness means grace and light and his dark side the terrible temptation of power. Man has already received so much knowledge that he can destroy his own planet. Let us hope that God's good spirit will guide him in his decisions, because it will depend on man's decision whether God's creation will continue. Nothing shows more drastically than this possibility how much of divine power has come within reach of man.[104]

JUNG AND GOD

When John Freeman asked Jung in a 1959 BBC interview if he believed in God, he answered, "I don't need to believe ... I know," thereby landing himself in controversy again. To correspondents he wrote:

> Mr. Freeman in his characteristic manner fired the question you allude to at me in a somewhat surprising way, so that I was perplexed and had to say the next thing which came into my mind. As soon as the answer had left the "edge of my teeth" I knew I had said something controversial, puzzling, or even ambiguous. I was therefore just waiting for letters like yours.[105]

> When I say that I don't need to believe in God because I "know," I mean I know of the existence of God-images in general and in particular. I know it is a matter of a universal experience and, in so far as I am no exception, I know that I have such experience also, which I call God. It is the experience of my will over against another and very often stronger will, crossing my path often with seemingly disastrous results, putting strange ideas into my head and maneuvering my fate sometimes into most undesirable corners or giving it unexpected favorable twists, outside my knowledge and my intention. The strange force against or for my conscious tendencies is well known to me. So I say: "I know Him." But why should you call this something "God?" I would ask: "Why not?" It has always been called "God."[106]

In his scientific writing, Jung always spoke of the "God-image," pointing to its universal manifestations. In correspondence and conversation, he made more direct and personal statements.

> I find that all my thoughts circle around God like the planets around the sun and are as irresistibly attracted by Him. I feel it would be the grossest sin if I were to oppose any resistance to this force.[107]

> The Divine Presence is more than anything else. There is more than one way to the rediscovery of the *genus divinum* in us. This is

Manjusri, Bodhisattva of Transcendental Wisdom; thanka painted on silk, Tibet,
c. seventeenth century.

Manjusri is dedicated to fearless proclamation of the Law. Jung felt strongly that he must
speak out about the religious aspects of self-knowledge.

Shuffle-shoon and Amberlocks;
painting by Maxfield Parrish, *c.* 1920.
Throughout his life Jung found natural
wisdom and creative answers when he
consulted with the child in himself.

the only thing that matters.... I wanted the proof of a living Spirit and I got it. Don't ask me at what a price.... I don't want to prescribe a way to other people, because I know that my way has been prescribed to me by a hand far above my reach. I know it all sounds so damned grand. I am sorry that it does, but I don't mean it. It is grand and I am only trying to be a decent tool and don't feel grand at all.[108]

Elizabeth Howes writes,

From the first moment I met him ... till the last time I saw him – when he said, "Go on talking about the religious aspects of my work. They are the most important parts" – I was involved in probing with him the whole religious process of individuation....

Regardless of what he tried to do in remaining scientific in his writing, when he talked to me face to face he left no doubt in my mind that when he spoke of God he was speaking of more than the archetype of God. This is sharply emphasized in a statement he made after he had been talking most movingly about the use and need of prayer. "Why do I have to talk about God? Because He is everywhere! I am only the spoon in His kitchen."[109]

In a letter to Laurens van der Post, Jung declares,

I cannot define for you what God is. I can only say that my work has proved empirically that the pattern of God exists in every man and that this pattern has at its disposal the greatest of all his energies for transformation and transfiguration of his natural being. Not only the meaning of his life but his renewal and his institutions depend on his conscious relationship with this pattern of his collective unconscious.[110]

But was there fusion with God? The *"unio mystica* with the potential world" – the third stage of conjunction written of but not experienced by the alchemists? A "synthesis of the conscious and unconscious?" Freedom from opposites?

In his last years there are hints in Jung's letters that his forehead still held back that millimeter from the floor.

Eastern philosophy fills a psychic lacuna in us but without answering the problem posed by Christianity. Since I am neither an Indian nor a Chinese, I shall probably have to rest content with my European presuppositions, otherwise I would be in danger of losing my roots for a second time. This is something I would rather not risk, for I know the price one has to pay to restore a continuity that has been lost.[111]

I cannot subscribe to your statements ... although they bring you perilously close to the ideal of Yoga: nirvana [freedom from the opposites]. I know those moments of liberation come flashing out of the process, but I shun them because I always feel at such a moment that I have thrown off the burden of being human and that it will fall back on me with redoubled weight.[112]

I tried to find the best truth and the clearest light I could attain to, and since I have reached my highest point I can't transcend any more, I am guarding my light and my treasure, convinced that nobody would gain and I myself would be badly, even hopelessly

The Pilgrim on the Road; woodcut, 1530.
Late letters and accounts by Jung bear witness to his continuing role as a pilgrim on the road between East and West.

injured, if I should lose it. It is most precious not only to me, but above all to the darkness of the creator, who needs man to illuminate His creation.[113]

Chilean diplomat and writer Miguel Serrano, who formed a late close relationship with Jung, observed:

Up until the last moment Jung still seemed to be searching. Perhaps his was the road of the Magician who, unlike the Saint, did not yearn for fusion or for the peace of God, but preferred the eternal highway with all its unhappiness. But I cannot be certain of that.[114]

For all that, Jung, living out the final patterns of his life, continued to feed cosmic answers to the small boy within himself who used to sit on a stone, wondering, "Am I the one who is sitting on the stone, or am I the stone on which he is sitting?"

In one dream, which I had in October 1958, I caught sight from my house of two lens-shaped metallically gleaming disks, which hurtled in a narrow arc over the house and down to the lake. They were two UFOs. Then another body came flying directly toward me. It was a perfectly circular lens, like the objective of a telescope. At a distance of four or five hundred yards it stood still for a moment, and then flew off. Immediately afterward, another came speeding through the air: a lens with a metallic extension which led to a box – a magic lantern. At a distance of sixty or seventy yards it stood still in the air, pointing straight at me. I awoke with a feeling of astonishment. Still half in the dream, the thought passed through my head: "We always think the UFOs are projections of ours. Now it turns out that we are their projections. I am projected by the magic lantern as C.G. Jung. But who manipulates the apparatus?"

I had dreamed once before of the problem of the self and the ego. In that earlier dream I was on a hiking trip. I was walking along a little road through a hilly landscape; the sun was shining and I had a wide view in all directions. Then I came to a small wayside chapel. The door was ajar, and I went in. To my surprise there was no image of the Virgin on the altar, and no crucifix either, but only a wonderful flower arrangement. But then I saw that on the floor in front of the altar, facing me, sat a yogi – in lotus posture, in deep meditation. When I looked at him more closely, I realized that he had my face. I started in profound fright, and awoke with the thought: "Aha, so he is the one who is meditating me. He has a dream, and I am it." I knew that when he awakened, I would no longer be....

The aim of both these dreams is to effect a reversal of the relationship between ego-consciousness and the unconscious, and to represent the unconscious as the generator of the empirical personality. This reversal suggests that in the opinion of the "other side," our unconscious existence is the real one and our conscious world a kind of illusion, an apparent reality constructed for a specific purpose, like a dream which seems a reality as long as we are in it. It is clear that this state of affairs resembles very closely the Oriental concept of Maya.[115]

Seated Figure of Bodhidharma; porcelain, Chinese, Ming Dynasty, seventeenth century. Bodhidharma was an Indian sage who brought Buddhism into China. This figurine is a meditative aid. By sitting in the same position and gazing upon the figure of the Bodhidharma, one can see one's own inner state.

LAST WORK

Man and His Symbols, Jung's last work, had a typical birth. The highly successful Freeman interview prompted a publisher's request for a book of Jung's "more important and basic ideas," this time "for the people in the market place." No, said eighty-three-year-old Jung. He had never tried to popularize his work; anyway he was "old and rather tired."

Then he had a dream, which he told to John Freeman.

> Jung dreamed that, instead of sitting in his study and talking to the great doctors and psychiatrists who used to call on him from all over the world, he was standing in a public place and addressing a multitude of people who were listening to him with rapt attention and understanding what he said.[116]

Inner instinct was heeded and the publisher's second request was accepted. Jung's contribution to the book was completed only ten days before his death, "his legacy to the broad reading public," wrote John Freeman, from "one of the great doctors of all time and one of the great thinkers of this century."

Christ and the Wise Virgins; stone portal, Germany.
At eighty-three, Jung had a dream in which he addressed a multitude of ordinary people who listened with rapt attention and understanding. This prompted him to agree to the publication of his last book, *Man and His Symbols*.

SMALL COMFORT

That Jung felt his voice was too little heard and even less understood in his time is clear from letters of the last couple of years to the few who did bring him succor. Swiss political economist Professor Eugen Bohler attempted in many publications to apply Jung's ideas to a more comprehensive economic science and later wrote an introduction to a paperback anthology of Jung's writings.

Jung sent greetings.

> To you, dear friend ... for this dawning decade 1960–70, in whose lap the black-and-white cards of our uncertain fate await us. The past decade dealt me heavy blows – the death of dear friends and the even more painful loss of my wife, the end of my scientific activity and the burdens of old age, but also all sorts of honors and above all your friendship, which I value the more highly because it appears that men cannot stand me in the long run. Since I do not deem myself God-almighty enough to have made them other than they are, I must put it down entirely to my own account and lengthen my shadow accordingly. Your understanding and your interest have done much to restore my self-confidence, severely shaken by my incessant struggle with difficult contemporaries. It is indeed no trifling thing to be granted the happy proof that somehow one is "possible" and has achieved something whose meaning someone else, apart from myself, is able to see. Being well known not to say "famous" means little when one realizes that those who mouth my name have fundamentally no idea of what it's all about. The gratification of knowing that one is essentially posthumous is short-lived.[117]

The Catholic Mother Prioress of a contemplative order wrote to Jung of the great influence his writings had on herself and her community – around the time when Jung was complaining that he had written so frequently on religion that "I have been alternately accused of agnosticism, atheism, materialism and mysticism."

Jung replied,

> Rev. Mother Prioress,
> I am very grateful for the spiritual help you extend to me. I am in need of it with this gigantic misunderstanding which surrounds

me. All the riches I seem to possess are also my poverty, my lonesomeness in the world. The more I seem to possess, the more I stand to lose, when I get ready to approach the dark gate. I did not seek my life with its failures and accomplishments. It came to me with a power not my own. Whatever I have acquired serves a purpose I have not foreseen. Everything had to be shed and nothing remains my own. I quite agree with you: it is not easy to reach utmost poverty and simplicity. But it meets you, unbidden, on the way to the end of this existence.[118]

Jung now described himself as "an eighty-five-year-old ruin of a formerly capable man." In honor of what was to be his last birthday, Sir Herbert Read, art historian and writer, published a critique about Jung's ideas on the arts.
Jung wrote as thanks,

Dear Sir Herbert....
Your blessed words are the rays of a new sun over a sluggish swamp in which I felt buried. I often thought of Meister Eckhart, who was entombed for six hundred years, and asked myself time and again why there are no men in our epoch who could see at least what I was wrestling with. I think it is not mere vanity and desire for recognition on my part, but a genuine concern for my fellow-beings. It is presumably the ancient functional relationship of the medicine-man to his tribe, the participation mystique and the essence of the physician's ethos. I see the suffering of mankind in the individual's predicament and vice versa.[119]

In January 1961, Jung received confirmation of himself from an unexpected quarter with a belated letter of thanks from William Wilson, "Bill W," co-founder of Alcoholics Anonymous. In it he acknowledged how Jung's remarks to a chronically alcoholic patient, Rowland H., in 1931 – that his situation was hopeless unless "he could become the subject of a spiritual or religious experience, in short a genuine conversion" – had been instrumental in Bill W's own conversion and cure, leading to the foundation of Alcoholics Anonymous in 1934.
The long account concluded:

As you will now clearly see, this astonishing chain of events actually started long ago in your consulting room, and it was directly founded upon your own humility and deep perception.

Angel of Mercy of the Graveyard; marble sculpture, Vieques, Puerto Rico, early twentieth century. Photograph by M. Klaus.

On the death of an estranged friend, Jung, in the last decade of his life, wrote: "The hidden mystery of life is always hidden between Two, and it is the true mystery which cannot be betrayed by words or depleted by arguments."[120]

Very many thoughtful A.A.'s are students of your writings. Because of your conviction that man is something more than intellect, emotion, and two dollars worth of chemicals, you have especially endeared yourself to us.[121]

Jung's response was illuminating.

Dear Mr. W....
Those days I had to be exceedingly careful of what I said. I had found out that I was misunderstood in every possible way. Thus I was very careful when I talked to Rowland H. But what I really thought about was the result of many experiences with men of his kind.

His craving for alcohol was the equivalent, on a low level, of the spiritual thirst of our being for wholeness, expressed in medieval language: the union with God.

Bottle Spirit; photograph by Peter Angelo Simon, 1995.

Jung knew the craving for "spirits" could also be, unconsciously, the spiritual thirst and yearning for a deeper union with God.

How could one formulate such an insight in a language that is not misunderstood in our days?

The only right and legitimate way to such an experience is that it happens to you in reality, and it can only happen to you when you walk on a path which leads you to higher understanding....

I am strongly convinced that the evil principle prevailing in this world leads the unrecognized spiritual need into perdition if it is not counteracted either by real religious insight or by the protective wall of human community. An ordinary man, not protected by an action from above and isolated in society, cannot resist the power of evil which is called, very aptly, the Devil. But the use of such words arouses so many mistakes that one can only keep aloof from them as much as possible....

I am risking it with you because I conclude from your very decent and honest letter that you have acquired a point of view above the misleading platitudes one usually hears about alcoholism.

You see, "alcohol" in Latin is *spiritus*, and you use the same word for the highest religious experience as well as for the most depraving poison. The helpful formula therefore is: *spiritus contra spiritum.*

Thanking you again for your kind letter, I remain,

Yours sincerely,

C.G. Jung[122]

SELF-ASSESSMENT

The old man who said "I stand isolated between the faculties" wasn't given to see the degree to which he had already shifted the furniture in people's minds in the humanities, sciences, religions, arts, and everyday human behavior. Nor could he foresee his ever-present influence on the Human Potential Movement and Transpersonal Psychology, on universalists like mythologist Joseph Campbell or Franz Alt, who acknowledged his recognition of "religion as dynamite and not opium through him."

But Jung always knew at heart that his life, if understood, pointed a way.

> If I ask the value of my life, I can only measure myself against the centuries and then I must say, Yes, it means something. Measured by the ideas of today, it means nothing.[123]

> The difference between most people and myself is that for me the "dividing walls" are transparent. That is my peculiarity. Others find these walls so opaque that they see nothing behind them

and therefore think nothing is there. To some extent I perceive the processes going on in the background, and that gives me an inner certainty. People who see nothing have no certainties and can draw no conclusions – or do not trust them even if they do.[124]

In each aeon there are at least a few individuals who understand what man's real task consists of, and keep its tradition for future generations and a time when insight has reached a deeper and more general level. First the way of a few will be changed and in a few generations there will be more ... whoever is capable of such insight, no matter how isolated he is, should be aware of the law of synchronicity. As the old Chinese saying goes: "The right man sitting in his house and thinking the right thought will be heard a hundred miles away."[125]

Wang Hsi-chih Watching Geese; detail from painted handscroll by Ch'ien Hsuan, thirteenth century, China.

RETURN TO SOURCE

On May 6, 1961, too frail for his daily walk, Jung was driven around some of his favorite roads, saying goodbye to the countryside. Three separate wedding processions stopped the car's progress. Synchronicity, decided Jung, announcing his impending marriage to death. Four days later, Miguel Serrano was one of his last visitors. Jung received him in his study dressed in a "Japanese ceremonial gown, his Gnostic ring on his left hand, Teilhard de Chardin's book *The Human Phenomenon*, 'a great book,' by his side."

Serrano reports being "once again struck by the magnificent rigor of Jung's mind" in that conversation.

> Today no one pays attention to what lies behind words ... to the basic ideas that are there. Yet the idea is the only thing that is truly there. What I have done in my work, is simply to give new names to those ideas, to those realities. Consider, for example, the word "Unconscious." I have just finished reading a book by a Chinese Zen Buddhist. And it seemed to me that we were talking about the same thing, and that the only difference between us was that we gave different words to the same reality. Thus use of the word Unconscious doesn't matter; what counts is the idea that lies behind the word.[126]

Two slight strokes confined him to bed for a week. Marie-Louise von Franz was a visitor.

> When I last saw him he had a vision. "I see enormous stretches devastated, enormous stretches of the earth. But thank God it's not the whole planet."[127]

Three days before he died, Jung dispatched his son Franz to his cellar, saying, "Let's have a really good wine tonight."
Ruth Bailey later wrote to Miguel Serrano,

> For two days before he died he was away in some far country and he saw wonderful and beautiful things, I am sure of that. He smiled often and was happy ... he told me of the wonderful dream he had had; he said: "Now I know the truth but there is a

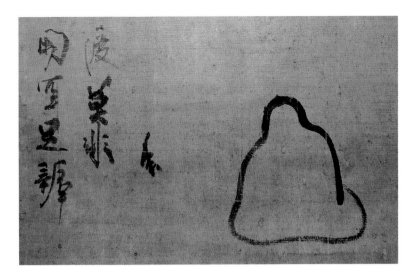

Meditating Daruma Facing the Wall; inkbrush painting, Nobutada (1565–1614), Japan. The calligraphy reads, "Quietness and emptiness are enough/to pass through life without error."

Jung realized he had given new names to realities known to other cultural systems. Chinese Zen Buddhism refers to the knowledge of the unconscious in terms similar to Jung's constructs. "What counts is the idea that lies behind the word."

small piece not filled in and when I know that I shall be dead." Also after that he had a wonderful dream which he told me in the night. He saw a huge round block of stone sitting on a high plateau and at the foot of the stone was engraved these words: "And this shall be a sign unto you of Wholeness and Oneness."[128]

At 4 p.m. on June 6, 1961, Jung died very peacefully, surrounded by his family. Not surprisingly, synchronicity accompanied his death. Laurens van der Post, on a voyage from Africa to Europe, reported a dream at the time he died of Jung waving goodbye. Barbara Hannah told how, minutes before his death, she discovered the relatively fresh battery in her car had completely run down. Nature joined in a couple of hours later with a freak storm over Küsnacht in which lightning struck and scarred the tree where Jung used to sit in the garden.

Jungian analyst June Singer was then studying at the Institute.

I never saw him during his lifetime.... On the day after his death I was one of a few trainees who went sorrowfully to Küsnacht.... The front door was open. I went in and waited in the fabled library, now hushed. A woman I did not know motioned me toward the stairway and I understood I was to go up alone. One door stood ajar in the upstairs hall. I entered the darkened room, lit only by two flickering candles in tall candlesticks on either side of the bed. There on the bed lay the waxen figure of the great man, so slender, so frail, seeming to be so small, almost transparent, peacefully at rest in his old-fashioned white nightshirt. A powerful presence pervaded the room and I stood there for a long moment, allowing the cool and glowing silence to penetrate my being. Then I turned and walked slowly down the stairs.[129]

Carl Gustav Jung was buried in Küsnacht cemetery. The family gravestone, designed by him, has inscribed on the top and bottom borders:

Vocatus atque non vocatus deus aderit
Invoked or not invoked, the god will be present

On the right and left sides is carved, from the First Epistle to the Corinthians:

Primus homo de terra terrenus
Secundus homo de caelo caelestis
The first man is of the earth and is earthly,
The second man is of heaven and is heavenly.

The prologue of Jung's "autobiography" sums up his story:

Life has always seemed to me like a plant that lives on its rhizome. Its true life is invisible, hidden in the rhizome. The part that appears above ground lasts only a single summer. Then it withers away – an ephemeral apparition. When we think of the unending growth and decay of life and civilizations, we cannot escape the impression of absolute nullity. Yet I have never lost a sense of something that lives and endures underneath the eternal flux. What we see is the blossom, which passes. The rhizome remains.[130]

Untitled; photograph by Jerry Uelsmann, 1964.

NOTES

Abbreviations of frequently cited works:

CW: *The Collected Works of C.G. Jung* (London: Routledge and Kegan Paul, 1964).

F/J: *The Freud/Jung Letters*, edited by William McGuire (London: Hogarth Press and Routledge and Kegan Paul, 1974).

JET: *C.G. Jung, Emma Jung and Toni Wolff*, edited by Ferne Jensen with assistance from Sidney Mullen (San Francisco: The Analytic Psychology Club of San Francisco, Inc., 1982).

L1: *C.G. Jung Letters, Volume I*, selected and edited by Gerhard Adler in collaboration with Aniela Jaffé (London: Routledge and Kegan Paul, 1972).

L2: *C.G. Jung Letters, Volume II*, selected and edited by Gerhard Adler in collaboration with Aniela Jaffé (Bollingen Series; Princeton: Princeton University Press, 1953)

MDR: *Memories, Dreams, Reflections* by C.G. Jung, recorded and edited by Aniela Jaffé (New York: Vintage Books, 1989).

Part One – Wounded

1. JET, pp. 51–52.
2. L1, p. 377, letter to P.W. Martin.
3. L1, p. 19, footnote.
4. L2, p. 408, letter to Anonymous.
5. MDR, p. 8.
6. MDR, pp. 17–18.
7. Wehr, Gerhard, *Jung: A Biography* (Boston: Shambhala, 1987), pp. 29–30.
8. MDR, pp. 9–10.
9. MDR, pp. 11–12.
10. MDR, pp. 13–15 and 23.
11. MDR, p. 15.
12. MDR, p. 19.
13. MDR, pp. 21–22.
14. MDR, pp. 36–42.

15. MDR, pp. 52, 50.

16. MDR, pp. 42–43.

17. Wehr, *Jung, op. cit.*, pp. 58–59.

18. MDR p. 99.

19. Wehr *op. cit.*, p. 74.

20. Jaffé, Aniela, *From the Life and Work of C.G. Jung* (Einsiedeln: Daimon, 1989), p. 2.

21. MDR, pp. 72–73.

22. MDR, pp. 108–109.

23. MDR, p. 114.

24. MDR, p. 127.

25. MDR, p. 131.

26. MDR, p. 117.

27. Wehr, *Jung, op. cit.*, p. 91.

28. MDR, p. 370, Appendix 2.

29. MDR, p. 367.

30. F/J, pp. 4–5.

31. F/J, p. 5.

32. MDR, pp. 149–150.

33. Jacobi, Jolande, Oral History Project, cited in *Uncovering Lives: The Uneasy Alliance of Biography and Psychology* by Alan C. Elins (New York: Oxford University Press, 1994), pp. 68–69.

34. F/J, pp. 94–95.

35. F/J, pp. 96–97.

36. F/J, p. 325.

37. F/J, pp. 181, 183.

38. F/J, p. 184.

39. F/J, pp. 199–200.

40. F/J, p. 200.

41. F/J, p. 208.

42. F/J, p. 212.

43. F/J, p. 207.

44. F/J, p. 228.

45. F/J, pp. 230–231.

46. F/J, p. 236.

47. MDR, pp. 155–156.

48. F/J, pp. 218–220.

49. MDR, pp. 150–151.

50. MDR, p. 158.

51. F/J, p. 452.

52. F/J, pp. 456–457.

53. F/J, p. 467.

54. F/J, p. 509.

55. F/J, p. 510.

56. F/J, p. 516.

57. F/J, p. 524.

58. F/J, pp. 525–526.

59. F/J, p. 534.

60. F/J, pp. 534–535.

61. F/J, pp. 538–539.

62. MDR, pp. 167–168.

63. MDR, pp. 170, 173–175.

64. MDR, pp. 175–176.

65. MDR, pp. 176–179.

66. MDR, pp. 179–182.

67. MDR, p. 189.

68. F/J, p.440.

69. Hannah, Barbara, *Jung: His Life and Work* (Boston: Shambhala, 1991), p. 120.

70. van der Post, Laurens, *Jung and the Story of Our Time* (New York: Random House, 1975), p. 177.

71. Hannah, *Jung, op. cit.*, p. 119.

72. MDR, pp. 182–183.

73. MDR, pp. 183–184.

74. MDR, pp. 184–185.

75. MDR, p. 188.

76. MDR, pp. 190–192.

77. Serrano, Miguel, *C.G. Jung and Herman Hesse: A Record of Two Friendships* (London: Routledge and Kegan Paul, 1966), pp. 94–95.

78. MDR, pp. 195–196.

79. MDR, pp. 192, 199.

Part Two – Healer

1. JET, p. 67.

2. Jaffé, *From the Life and Work, op. cit.*, p. 167.

3. L2, p. 323, letter to Henry A. Murray.

4. L2, p. 316, letter to Elined Kotschnig.

5. L2, p. 474, letter to A. Tjoa and R.H.C. Janssen.

6. JET, p. 39.
7. JET, p. 17.
8. MDR, p. 240.
9. MDR, pp. 247–248, 251–252.
10. MDR, pp. 255–256.
11. MDR, pp. 224–226, 237.
12. F/J, p. 294.
13. MDR, p. 340.
14. McGuire, William and Hull, R.F.C., editors, *C.G. Jung Speaking* (London and New York: Thames and Hudson, 1978), p. 348.
15. MDR, p. 205.
16. MDR, p. 209.
17. L1, p. 87, letter to A. Vetter.
18. JET, p. 97.
19. Hannah, *Jung, op. cit.*, p.74.
20. MDR, p. 145.
21. JET, pp. 51–52.
22. JET, p. 98.
23. L2, pp. 276–277, letter to Theodor Bovet.
24. JET, p. 120.
25. L2, p. 481, letter to Traugott Egloff.
26. L2, p. 402, letter to Anonymous.
27. Brome Vincent, *Jung: Man and Myth* (London: HarperCollins, 2001), pp. 212–213.
28. CW 10, "Civilization in Transition," p. 125.
29. L1, pp. 82–83, letter to Count Hermann Keyserling.
30. L1, pp. 108–109, letter to Anonymous.
31. L1, p. 239, letter to Anonymous.
32. Wilhelm, Richard, translator, *The Secret of the Golden Flower* (London: Routledge and Kegan Paul, 1974), p. 126.
33. Wilhelm, *The Secret, op. cit.*, p. 126.
34. JET, pp. 111–112.
35. L1, p. 375, letter to Olga Frobe–Kapteyn.
36. L2, pp. 258–259, letter to Pastor Walter Bernet.
37. L1, p. 236, letter to Aniela Jaffé.
38. JET, p. 119.
39. JET, p. 112.
40. L1, p. 59, letter to Anonymous.
41. JET, p. 103.

42. MDR, p. 133.

43. van der Post, *Jung, op. cit.*, p. 128.

44. van der Post, *Jung, op. cit.*, pp. 121–122.

45. JET, pp. 103–104.

46. Jaffé, *From the Life and Work, op. cit.*, pp. 106–107.

47. Wehr, *Jung, op. cit.*, p. 329.

48. JET, pp. 99–100.

49. MDR, p. 144.

50. JET, pp. 104–105.

51. LI, p. 41, letter to Oscar A.H. Schmitz.

52. LI, p. 422, letter to J. Allen Gilbert.

53. LI, p. 133, letter to Frau V.

54. JET, p. 75.

55. van der Post, *Jung, op. cit.*, p. 4.

56. LI, p. 561, letter to Sibylle Birkhauser-Oeri.

57. JET, pp. 50–51.

58. JET, pp. 47–48.

59. JET, pp. 32–33.

60. McGuire and Hull, *C.G. Jung Speaking, op. cit.*, pp. 50–51.

61. Hannah, *Jung, op. cit.*, p. 199.

62. JET, pp. 116–117.

63. Jaffé, *From the Life and Work, op. cit.*, p. 113.

64. JET, p. 98.

65. LI, p. 86, letter to Anonymous.

66. LI, p. 135, letter to Poul Bjerre.

67. LI, pp. 145–146, letter to Walter Cimbal.

68. CW 10, p. 534.

69. CW 10, pp. 538–541.

70. LI, p. 157, letter to E. Beit von Speyer.

71. LI, pp. 154–155, letter to Dr. B. Cohen.

72. LI, p. 162, letter to James Kirsch.

73. L2, p. xxxiv, letter to Henry A. Murray.

74. LI, p. 404, letter to J.H. van der Hoop, January 14, 1946.

75. Hannah, *Jung, op. cit.*, p. 269.

76. LI, p. 276, letter to Esther Harding.

77. MDR, pp. 275–277.

78. MDR, p. 277.

79. CW 10, "What India Can Teach Us," par. 1013.

80. MDR, pp. 282–283.

Part Three – Of the Soul

1. L2, p. 580, letter to Earl of Sandwich.
2. MDR, pp. 210–211.
3. Hannah, *op. cit., Jung*, pp. 264–265.
4. L1, p. 285, notes.
5. L1, pp. 285–286, letter to H.G. Baynes.
6. MDR, pp. 289–296.
7. L1, p. 343, letter to Anonymous.
8. Hannah, *Jung, op. cit.*, p. 283.
9. L1, pp. 424–425, letter to Eugene H. Henley.
10. L1, p. 442, letter to Ernst Anderes.
11. L1, p. 443, letter to Jolande Jacobi.
12. Brome, *Jung, op. cit.*, p. 213.
13. L1, p. 377, letter to P.W. Martin.
14. Wehr, *Jung, op. cit.*, p. 292.
15. JET, pp. 37–38.
16. JET, p. 118.
17. L1, p. 516, letter to Alwine von Keller.
18. L1, p. 568, letter to Hanna Oeri.
19. JET, p. 124.
20. Wehr, *Jung, op. cit.*, p. 377.
21. MDR, p. 233.
22. L2, p. 137, letter to Fr. Victor White.
23. MDR, p. 297.
24. MDR, pp. 218–220.
25. L2, pp. 20, 112, 115, letters to Aniela Jaffé, Jacob Amstutz, Henry Corbin.
26. CW 11, *Answer to Job*, p. 357.
27. L2, pp. 155–156, letter to Rev. Erastus Evans.
28. L2, pp. 72–73, letter to Fr. Victor White.
29. L2, pp. 435–436, letter to Rev. Morton T. Kelsey.
30. CW 11, *Answer to Job*, p. 417.
31. CW 11, *Answer to Job*, p. 470.
32. L1, p. 127, letter to Paul Maag.
33. L1, p. 66, letter to Walter Robert Corti.
34. L1, p. 392, letter to Pastor H. Wagmann.
35. L2, p. 436, letter to Rev. Morton Kelsey.
36. L2, pp. 76–77, letter to Dorothee Hoch.
37. L1, p. 96, letter to Anonymous.

38. L2, p. 183, letter to Anonymous.

39. L2, p. 4, letter to Heinrich Boltze.

40. L2, p. 77, letter to Dorothee Hoch.

41. L1, p. 520, letter to Jurg Fierz.

42. Essay by Pastor Bernet, 1966.

43. L2, p. 242, letter to Fr. Victor White.

44. L2, pp. 108–109, letter to Carl Seelig.

45. McGuire and Hull, *C.G. Jung Speaking, op. cit.,* pp. 325, 378.

46. L1, pp. 174–175, letter to Wolfgang Pauli.

47. Jaffé, *From the Life and Work, op. cit.,* p. 166.

48. L2, p. 308, letter to Professor Nelson.

49. McGuire and Hull, *C. G .Jung Speaking, op. cit.,* p. 387.

50. L1, p. 548, letter to Edward Whitmont.

51. CW 14, *Mysterium Coniunctionis,* par. 662.

52. Jung, C.G. and Pauli, W., *The Interpretation of Nature and the Psyche* (London: Routledge and Kegan Paul, 1955), p. 7.

53. L2, pp. 398–400, letter to Stephen Abrams.

54. JET, p. 3.

55. McGuire and Hull, *C.G. Jung Speaking, op. cit.,* p. 402.

56. JET, p. 41.

57. JET, p. 7.

58. MDR, p. 225.

59. L2, p. 117, letter to James Kirsch.

60. L2, p. 121, letter to Countess Elizabeth Klinckowstroem.

61. Hannah, *Jung, op. cit.,* p. 313.

62. L2, pp. 424–425, letter to Dr. Daniel Brody.

63. Serrano, Miguel, *C.G. Jung and Herman Hesse, op. cit.,* pp. 60–61.

64. Jaffé, Aniela, editor, with Adler, Gerhard, *C.G. Jung Briefe* (Walther Verlag AG Ohten, 1972–73), p. 386.

65. L2, p. 171, letter to Fr. Victor White.

66. Uhsadel, Walther, *Evangelische Seelsorge* (Heidelberg: Quelle and Meyer, 1966), p. 121.

67. Jaffé, *From the Life and Work, op. cit.,* p. 100.

68. Hannah, *Jung, op. cit.,* p. 323.

69. L2, p. 270, letter to Mary Bancroft.

70. JET, p. 120.

71. JET, p. 34.

72. L2, p. 251, letter to Fr. Victor White.

73. JET, p. 95.

74. L2, p. 284, letter to Erich Neumann.
75. Brome, *Jung, op. cit.*, p. 260.
76. MDR, p. 296.
77. L2, p. 316, letter to Marianne Niehus-Jung.
78. van der Post, *Jung, op. cit.*, p. 177.
79. L2, p. 299, letter to Eugen Bohler; p. 233, letter to Manfred Bleuler.
80. MDR, p. 356.
81. *A Matter of Heart* film transcript, James Kirsch.
82. *Die Gesammelten Werke von C.G. Jung*, "The Psychology of the Transference," (Zürich: Rascher, 1958–1970), pp. 178–179.
83. CW 14, *Mysterium Coniunctionis*, Vol. 2, pars. 760, 762, 767–771.
84. Brome, *Jung, op. cit.*, p. 257.
85. Jaffé, *From the Life and Work, op. cit.*, pp. 101, 114–115.
86. JET, p. 126.
87. L1, p. 542, letter to Serge Moreux.
88. McGuire and Hull, *C.G. Jung Speaking, op. cit.*, p. 249.
89. JET, p. 16.
90. MDR, p. 225.
91. L2, p. 351, letter to Aniela Jaffé.
92. L2, p. 88, letter to Karl Oftinger.
93. L2, p. 363, letter to Gustav Schmaltz.
94. MDR, pp. vii–viii.
95. MDR, p. xii.
96. JET, pp. 114–116.
97. Wehr, Gerhard, *An Illustrated Biography of C.G. Jung* (Boston: Shambhala, 1989), p. 143.
98. Interview with Richard Evans, 1957.
99. Jung, C.G., "Essay on Contemporary Events."
100. CW 10, *The Meaning of Psychology for Modern Man*, p. 149.
101. CW 10, *The Undiscovered Self*, pp. 304–305.
102. CW 11, *Answer to Job*, p. 459.
103. CW 10, *The Undiscovered Self*, p. 258.
104. L2, p. 316, letter to Elined Kotschnig.
105. L2, p. 525, letter to M. Leonard.
106. L2, p. 522, letter to Valentine Brooke.
107. L2, p. 236, letter to Pater Lucas Menz.
108. L1, pp. 491–492, letter to Fr. Victor White.
109. JET, p. 120.
110. van der Post, *Jung, op. cit.*, p. 216.

111. L2, p. 121, letter to Countess Elizabeth Klinckowstroem.

112. L2, p. 238, letter to Pater Lucas Menz.

113. L2, p. 597, letter to Miguel Serrano.

114. *C.G. Jung and Herman Hesse*, Serrano, *op. cit.*, p. 112.

115. MDR, pp. 323–324.

116. Jung, C.G., editor, *Man and His Symbols*, introduction (London: Aldus Books, 1964), p. 10.

117. L2, pp. 529–530, letter to Eugen Bo; p. 566, letter to Rev. Kenneth Gordon Lafleur.

118. L2, p. 516, letter to Mother Prioress of a contemplative order.

119. L2, pp. 586–589, letter to Sir Herbert Read.

120. L2, p. 581, letter to Mother Prioress.

121. "The Bill W./Carl Jung Letters," A.A.'s *Grapevine*, 1963, 1968, 1974.

122. *Ibid.*

123. MDR, p. xii.

124. MDR, pp. 355–356.

125. L2, p. 595, letter to Miguel Serrano.

126. Serrano, *C.G. Jung and Herman Hesse*, *op. cit.*, p. 100.

127. von Franz, Marie-Louise, *C.G. Jung: His Myth in Our Time* (New York: C.G. Jung Foundation Publications, 1975)

128. Serrano, *C.G. Jung and Herman Hesse*, *op. cit.*, p. 104.

129. JET, p. 83.

130. MDR, p. 4.

INDEX

the unconscious, 41, 69–71, 95, 96
  and alchemy, 99
  and individuation, 105–18
  and synchronicity, 187, 190
  synthesis of the consciousness with, 217
  see also collective unconscious
United States
  Jung's visits to, 48, 48, 59–60, 101
  World conference of psychologists (1909), 48, 48
Unus Mundus
  and synchronicity, 193–4

van der Post, Sir Laurens, 196, 196, 212, 232–3, 245
Velarde, Pablita
  Eagle Dancer, 90
visions and fantasies, 69–71, 74–6
  following Jung's heart attack, 153–9
  Ka, 75, 75–6
  mystical marriage, 157–8, 214–15
  Philemon, 74, 74–6
  Salome and Elijah, 71
  Siegfried, 70–1
  Vision of 1914 (painting by Jung), 228

Wandjina Aboriginal Australian rock art, 159
Wang Hsi chih Watching Geese (Ch'ien Hsuan), 242–3
Wasserman, James & Nancy
  Kabbalistic Tree of Life, 184
Watts, Alan, 127
Wells, H.G., 138, 196
Wheelwright, Jane
  reminiscences of, 101, 104, 117–20, 122, 124
Wheelwright, Joseph, 123
White, Father Victor, 174, 183, 205, 210
Wilson, William ("Bill W."), 238–41
Wolf Devouring the King (Maier), 113
Wolff, Toni, 72, 73, 128, 129–32, 130, 212, 214
  as an analyst, 129–30
  at Bollingen, 135
  death, 199–201

and Emma Jung, 73, 131, 131–2, 201
publication of writings, 201–2
Studies in Jungian Psychology, 202
women and the anima, 71, 107, 107–10, 112, 125
word association, 43
World conference of psychologists (Massachusetts), 48, 48
The Worship of the Scarab, 188

Yoggi (Jung's dog), 102–4
Young Woman in Garden (Cassatt), 121
Yudovin, Solomon
  Funeral (woodcut), 143

Zausner, Tobi
  Memories (oil painting), 111
Zürich
  C.G. Jung Institute, 128, 162, 163, 197
  Jung's work at Burghölzi Hospital, 43, 43–4
  Prize for Literature, 138
  Psychological Club, 128, 129, 135, 201, 202

SOURCES

TEXT CREDITS

Adler, Gerhard and Aniela Jaffé, editors, *C.G. Jung Letters, Volume I*. Copyright © 1972 Princeton University Press and Taylor & Francis Books UK, formerly International Thompson/Routledge. Reprinted by permission of Princeton University Press. Reproduced by permission of Taylor & Francis Books UK.

Adler, Gerhard, and Aniela Jaffé, editors, C.G. *Jung Letters, Volume II*. Copyright © 1953 Princeton University Press and Taylor & Francis Books UK, formerly International Thompson/Routledge. Reprinted by permission of Princeton University Press. Reproduced by permission of Taylor & Francis Books UK.

Brome, Vincent, *Jung: Man and Myth*. Copyright © 2001 House of Stratus, Looe.

Hannah, Barbara, *Jung: His Life and Work*. Copyright © 1991 Shambhala Publications, Boston. Reprinted by kind permission of Mrs. Marie-Louise von Franz and Dr. Emmanuel Kennedy.

Jaffé, Aniela, *From the Life and Work of C.G. Jung*. Copyright © 1989 Daimon, Einsiedeln. Reprinted by kind permission of Daimon Verlag.

Jensen, Ferne, editor, assisted by Sidney Mullen, *C.G. Jung, Emma Jung and Toni Wolff*. Copyright © 1982. Published by the Analytic Psychology Club of San Francisco and reprinted by their kind permission.

Jung, C.G., *The Collected Works of C.G. Jung*. CW 10, 11, 14, 16 copyright © 1977 Princeton University Press and Taylor & Francis Books UK, formerly International Thompson/Routledge. Reprinted by permission of Princeton University Press. Reproduced by permission of Taylor & Francis Books UK.

Jung, C.G., editor, *Man and His Symbols*. Copyright © 1964 Aldus Books Limited, London.

Jung, C.G., *Memories, Dreams, Reflections*, translated by Richard and Clara Winston, edited by Aniela Jaffe, translation copyright © 1961, 1962, 1963 and renewed 1989, 1990, 1991 by Random House LLC. Used by permission of Pantheon

PICTURE CREDITS

The publisher would like to thank the following people, museums, and photographic libraries for permission to reproduce their material. Every care has been taken to trace copyright holders. However, if we have omitted anyone we apologise and will, if informed, make corrections to any future edition.

Page 2 Harley Ms. 3469. Copyright © British Library, London
20 Private Collection, Basel. Courtesy of Gallerie Bruno Bischofberger, Zürich
22 Photo courtesy of K. Mann Library, NY
24(a) Copyright © 2007 Foundation of the Works of C.G. Jung, Zürich
24(b) Copyright © 2007 Foundation of the Works of C.G. Jung, Zürich
26 Photo copyright © 1981 Rosalie Winard, NY
27 Vatican Museums/Scala/Art Resource, NY/ © ADAGP, Paris and DACS, London 2011
28 Herscovici/Art Resource, NY/ © ADAGP, Paris and DACS, London 2011
29 Copyright © Landesmuseum, Stuttgart, Germany
30 Copyright © 2007 Foundation of the Works of C.G. Jung, Zürich
31 Courtesy of the artist, Morris Graves. Photo by Paul McCapia
32 Copyright © Brooklyn Museum, NY, gift of Mr. and Mrs. M. Lowenthal through the Roebling Society (68.160)
33 Copyright © 2007 Foundation of the Works of C.G. Jung, Zürich
35 Courtesy of the artist, Robert Taylor
37 Copyright © 2007 Foundation of the Works of C.G. Jung, Zürich
38 Musée d'Orsay, Paris/ Réunion des Musées Nationaux/Art Resource, NY
40 Private Collection/Scala/Art Resource, NY
41 Photo courtesy of Stefanie Preiswerk
42 Private Collection/Art Resource, NY/ © ADAGP, Paris and DACS, London 2011
43 Copyright © 2007 Foundation of the Works of C.G. Jung, Zürich
45 Copyright © 2007 Foundation of the Works of C.G. Jung, Zürich
47 Photo courtesy of K. Mann Library, NY
48 Clark University, Worcester, MA
50 Ms. Rhenaugiensis 172, fol.10v, Zentralbibliothek, Zürich. Courtesy of the library
52 Photo courtesy of K. Mann Library, NY
54 Image copyright © The Metropolitan Museum of Art/Image Source/Art Resource, NY
57 Photo courtesy of The Freud Museum, London

60 Photo courtesy of K. Mann Library, NY

64 Copyright © 1994, 1998 James Wasserman, from *The Egyptian Book of the Dead* (San Francisco: Chronicle Books). Courtesy of James Wasserman

66 Photo copyright © 1995 Peter Angelo Simon, NY, www.PeterAngeloSimon.com

68 Photo copyright © 1995 Peter Angelo Simon, NY, www.PeterAngeloSimon.com

70 Copyright © 2009 Foundation of the Works of C.G. Jung, Zürich. First published by W.W. Norton & Company

72 Photo courtesy of K. Mann Library, NY

74 The Pierpoint Morgan Library, NY/Art Resource, NY

75 From E.A.W. Budge, *Book of the Dead* (London: Keegan, Paul, 1899)

77 From C.W. King, *The Gnostics and their Remains*, 1887, in J. Wasserman, *Art & Symbols of the Occult* (Rochester, VT: Destiny Books, 1993)

79 Copyright © 2007 Foundation of the Works of C.G. Jung, Zürich, Copyright © Robert Hinshaw

80 Copyright © 2009 Foundation of the Works of C.G. Jung, Zürich. First published by W.W. Norton & Company

82 Photo courtesy of K. Mann Library, NY

83 Sistine Chapel, Vatican Palace/Scala/Art Resource, NY

84 Courtesy of the Bochum Museum, Germany/ © ADAGP, Paris and DACS, London 2011

86 Photo courtesy of K. Mann Library, NY

87 Courtesy of Dr. Debrunner

88 Pushkin Museum of Fine Arts, Moscow/Scala/Art Resource, NY/ © Succession Picasso/DACS, London 2011

89 Photo courtesy of Field Museum of Natural History, Chicago

90 Courtesy of School of American Research, Santa Fe, NM

93 Courtesy of the artist, Francesco Clemente and Anthony d'Offay Gallery, London

94(a) Photo copyright © Erbengemeinschaft C.G. Jung

94(b) Photo copyright © Erbengemeinschaft C.G. Jung

96 Copyright © 1994 Judith Margolis. Private Collection, Jerusalem

97 Image copyright © The Metropolitan Museum of Art/Image Source/Art Resource, NY

98 From Ernst & Johanna Lehner, *Devils, Demons & Witchcraft* (New York: Dover, 1971)

100 From E.A.W. Budge, *Gods of the Egyptians* (New York: Dover, 1904)

101 Photo courtesy of K. Mann Library, NY

102 Photo courtesy of K. Mann Library, NY

103 Image copyright © The Metropolitan Museum of Art/Image Source/Art Resource, NY

105 The Philadelphia Museum of Art/Art Resource, NY/ © ADAGP, Paris and DACS, London 2011

106 Copyright © 1991, Courtesy of the artist, Frank LaPena

107 Image copyright © The Metropolitan Museum of Art/Image Source/Art Resource, NY

108 Photo copyright © Clive Hicks

109 Image copyright © The Metropolitan Museum of Art/Image Source/Art Resource, NY

111 Copyright © 1981, courtesy of the artist, Tobi Zausner

112 Image copyright © The Metropolitan Museum of Art/Image Source/Art Resource, NY

113 Bibliothèque d'Arsenal, Paris/Snark/Art Resource, NY

114 Enzo by William Segal

115 Image copyright © The Metropolitan Museum of Art/Image Source/Art Resource, NY

117 Photo courtesy of K. Mann Library, NY

118 Image copyright © The Metropolitan Museum of Art/Image Source/Art Resource, NY

119 Minister of Cultural Affairs, Quebec

121 Musée d'Orsay, Paris/Erich Lessing/Art Resource, NY

122 Image copyright © The Metropolitan Museum of Art/Image Source/Art Resource, NY

124 Smithsonian American Art Museum, Washington DC/Art Resource, NY

125 Photo copyright © 1988 courtesy of Linda Connor

126 Image copyright © The Metropolitan Museum of Art/Image Source/Art Resource, NY

128 Photo courtesy of K. Mann Library, NY

130 Photo courtesy of K. Mann Library, NY

131 Photo courtesy of K. Mann Library, NY

132 Image copyright © The Metropolitan Museum of Art/Image Source/Art Resource, NY

133 Courtesy of Walther Niehus

134 Private Collection/photograph by Yousuf Karsh, Camera Press London

135 Private Collection, NY

137 Photo courtesy of K. Mann Library, NY

139 Photo courtesy of Prof. Dr. C.A. Meier, Zürich

141 Image copyright © The Metropolitan Museum of Art/Image Source/Art Resource, NY

142 Estate of R.B. Kitaj. Tate Gallery, London (MU 1943)/Art Resource, NY

143 Copyright © Israel Museum, Jerusalem

147 Copyright © Brooklyn Museum, NY, gift of Mr and Mrs R.L. Poster in honor of Dr. B.H. Schaffner (84.142)

148 Ajit Mookerjee Collection, India

149 Harley Ms. 3469. Copyright © British Library, London

150 Art Museum of Princeton University, Princeton. Copyright © Trustees of Princeton University

152 Courtesy of the artist, Francesco Clemente

153 Digital Image © The Museum of Modern Art/Scala/Art Resource, NY

154 Private Collection/Image Select/Art Resource, NY

155 Image copyright © The Metropolitan Museum of Art/Image Source/Art Resource, NY

157 Digital Image © The Museum of Modern Art/Scala/Art Resource, NY

158 From Franc Newcomb, *Shooting Chant* (New York: Dover, 1975)

159 From D. Mowaljarlai and J. Malnic, *Yorro Yorro* (Rochester, VT: Inner Traditions, 1993). Courtesy of the publisher

160 From Ernst & Johanna Lehner, *Devils, Demons & Witchcraft* (New York: Dover, 1971)

161 Photo courtesy of K. Mann Library, NY

162 Photo courtesy of Robert Johnson

163 Photo courtesy of Robert Johnson

165 Photo courtesy of K. Mann Library, NY

166 Photo copyright © Erbengemeinschaft C.G. Jung

167 Photo courtesy of K. Mann Library, NY

169 From Ernst & Johanna Lehner, *Devils, Demons & Witchcraft* (New York: Dover, 1971)

170 Copyright © Art Institute of Chicago, Illinois

171 From Ernst & Johanna Lehner, *Devils, Demons & Witchcraft* (New York: Dover, 1971)

173 Image copyright © The Metropolitan Museum of Art/Image Source/Art Resource, NY

175 Image copyright © The Metropolitan Museum of Art/Image Source/Art Resource, NY

176 Collection of Mr. & Mrs. Arthur G. Altshul. Photo by Christine Guest.

179 Private Collection/Foto Marburg/Art Resource, NY

182 Photo copyright © 1989 of Rosalie Winard

183 Private Collection, NY

184 Painting copyright © 1992, 1995 James and Nancy Wasserman

186 Photo courtesy of NASA

188 From E.A.W. Budge, *Life in Ancient Egypt* (New York: Dover, 1950)

190 Courtesy of the artist, Morris Graves, and Schmidt Bingham Gallery, NY

191 Copyright © 1995. Courtesy of Craig San Roche

192 Image copyright © The Metropolitan Museum of Art/Image Source/Art Resource, NY

195 Copyright © Joe Geshick

196 Photo courtesy of Mickey Lemle, Lemle Pictures

198 Biblioteca Statale, Lucca/Scala/Art Resource, NY

199 © Tate, London 2011/Art Resource, NY

200 Photo courtesy of K. Mann Library, NY

203 Private Collection, CA. Courtesy of Mrs. Alek Rapoport/The Bridgeman Art Library, London

204 Photo courtesy of K. Mann Library, NY

207 From Nik Douglas, *Tibetan Charms* (New York: Dover, 1978)

208 Photo courtesy of K. Mann Library, NY

209 Photo courtesy of K. Mann Library, NY

211 Photo copyright © Erbengemeinschaft C.G. Jung

213 Harley Ms. 3469. Copyright © British Library, London

214–15 Los Angeles County Museum of Art/Art Resource, NY

216 Los Angeles County Museum of Art/Art Resource, NY

218 Image copyright © The Metropolitan Museum of Art/Image Source/Art Resource, NY

220 Vatican Museums/Alinari/Art Resource, NY

221 Courtesy of the artist, Francesco Clemente

222 Photo courtesy of K. Mann Library, NY

223 Digital Image © The Museum of Modern Art/Scala/Art Resource, NY

225 Private Collection/Art Resource, NY

227 Copyright ©Alex Haas Studio, NY

228 Copyright © 2009 Foundation of the Works of C.G. Jung, Zürich. First published by W.W. Norton & Company

231 Image copyright © The Metropolitan Museum of Art/Image Source/Art Resource, NY

232 From Eugene Field, *Poems of Childhood* (New York: Scribners, 1932)/ © Maxfield Parrish/Licensed by ASaP and DACS, London/VAGA, New York 2011

235 Image copyright © The Metropolitan Museum of Art/Image Source/Art
  Resource, NY
236 Private Collection/Art Resource, NY
239 Photo copyright © 1990 M. Klaus
240 Photo copyright © 1995 Peter Angelo Simon, NY, www.PeterAngeloSimon.
  com
242–3 Image copyright © The Metropolitan Museum of Art/Image Source/Art
  Resource, NY
245 From Stephen Addis, *The Art of Zen* (New York: Abrams, 1989)
247 Photo copyright © Jerry Uelsmann

The editors would like to thank Alison Jasonides, Art Resource, NY; Annmari
Ronnberg, ARAS, The Jung Center of NY; and Michelle McKee, Khristine Mann
Library, The Jung Center of NY.

AUTHOR ACKNOWLEDGMENTS

For everyone involved in the writing and production of this book, it was a
"labor of love". This is as true of its first publication by Joe Kulin and the
company of Parabola, as it is of its present publisher Watkins, so ably assisted
by Sandra Rigby, Fiona Robertson, Luana Gobbo, Gail Jones, Billy Waqar
and staff.

My heartfelt thanks to Duncan Baird for undertaking this elegant edition for an
educational as well as general public readership.

Enduring thanks to Donald Rubin, whose belief in the book's merits initiated
it back into print; to Bruce Payne who oversaw co-operative assistance from the
Shelley & Donald Rubin Foundation in New York as co-publishers; to Joe Kulin as
persistent bridging agent and friend of the book; and to Olivier Bernier for his very
pertinent foreword.

Although the writing of this book was necessarily a loner's task on the outside,
its substance is derived from interaction with the huge presence of Carl Gustav Jung,
backed by the unfathomable Source of Life that inspires, and conspires with, each
of us to play our role in its service. In my case, as messenger, I have thankfully met
with allies along the way.

To Joseph Kulin, as publisher and abiding friend, I owe a special expression of gratitude for his persistent belief in my manuscript and taking the gamble on its publication.

Parabola's idea of presenting the text as an illustrated book added more to it than I could have dreamed of for myself. In addition, they gave me the rare opportunity to be included at each stage of production.

I'd like to pay tribute to art researcher Miriam Faugno, whose empathy of soul is visible in her choice of images; to designer Jim Wasserman's enthusiastic creation of an elegantly spare presentation; and to David Appelbaum's discriminating direction of the production assisted by the meticulous work of Natalie Baan and Shanti Fader.

I also wish to thank each of Parabola's staff for small personal gestures that helped this traveling stranger find a sense of family.

Without Pauline Thompson's financial endorsement this book could not have gone into production. Her hospitable, enlivening friendship is a bonus that I treasure.

Esteemed author and lecturer Olivier Bernier, who directs the Van Waveren Foundation, was the first to acknowledge the manuscript with a publication development grant. His additional underwriting of a promotional speaking tour has ensured the book's reach to a wider general audience than would otherwise have been possible.

Jean Houston, whose inspirational teaching ability and warm personality I've always admired, gave early active support for the text, and generously agreed to write an introduction in the midst of huge demands on her time.

In the project's earliest stages my soul friend Dr. Fred Kyneur lent me his library of Jung books for two patient years, and scholar Kenji Tanaka stoically initiated me into the maze of computer technology.

To each individual, and numerous others who have added pieces, professional and personal, to the overall tapestry, I acknowledge your contribution with deeply felt thanks.

Finally, to you as intended reader, I joyfully release this book on its journey into its own life.